This b

CH.

POLITICS AND OLD AGE

Two weddings and a baby

Politics and Old Age

Older citizens and political processes in Britain

JOHN A. VINCENT, GUY PATTERSON and KAREN WALE
*School of Historical, Political and Sociological Studies,
University of Exeter, UK*

Ashgate

Aldershot • Burlington USA • Singapore • Sydney

Published by
Ashgate Publishing Limited
Gower House
Croft Road
Aldershot
Hampshire GU11 3HR
England

Ashgate Publishing Company
131 Main Street
Burlington, VT 05401-5600 USA

Ashgate website: http://www.ashgate.com

British Library Cataloguing in Publication Data
Vincent, John, 1947 -
    Politics and old age : older citizens and political
    processes in Britain
    1. Aged - Great Britain - Political activity 2. Senior power
    - Great Britain
    I. Title II. Patterson, Guy III. Wale, Karen
    305.2'6'0941

Library of Congress Control Number: 2001093299

ISBN 0 7546 1756 4

Printed and bound in Great Britain by Biddles Ltd, *www.biddles.co.uk*

Contents

List of Charts

List of Tables

Acknowledgements

The authors would like gratefully to acknowledge the help of the Leverhulme Trust, which provided the grant to enable our research project to proceed. We acknowledge the help of the ESRC Data Archive and those researchers who have deposited with the archive surveys that we have used for our research. Their names are detailed in the Bibliography. Our thanks to the staff at MORI who helped us conduct our own survey and to Gail Prosser who copy-edited the manuscript. Sarah Vincent, Peter Smith and John Miles also made helpful comments and suggestions about the book.

Most particularly we wish to express our sincere thanks to the many people from all walks of life who gave their time to assist us and allowed us to interview them. Without their cooperation the book would not have been written.

List of Abbreviations

ABI	Association of British Insurers
AGM	Annual General Meeting
ARP/O50	Association of Retired People and Those over Fifty
BEM	Black and Ethnic Minority Elders' Working Group
BES	British Election Survey
BGOP	Better Government for Older People
BPTUAA	British Pensioners' Trade Union Action Association
DSS	Department of Social Security
EDM	Early Day Motion
EU	European Union
GLC	Greater London Council
GLF	Greater London Forum for the Elderly
GMB	General, Municipal and Boilermakers Union
IMG	Inter-Ministerial Group
MEBESA	Minority Ethnic Black Elders Strategic Alliance
MEP	Member of the European Parliament
MIG	Minimum Income Guarantee
MP	Member of Parliament
NAPF	National Association of Pension Funds
NFOAPA	National Federation of Old Age Pensions Associations
NHS	National Health Service
NPC	National Pensioners' Convention
NUM	National Union of Mineworkers
NUPE	National Union of Public Employees
NUR	National Union of Railwaymen
OPCS	Office of Population Census and Surveys
OPPOL	Older People and Politics Project
PAYG	Pay as You Go
PRC	Pensioners' Rights Campaign
SERPS	State Earnings Related Pension Scheme
TGWU	Transport and General Workers Union
TUC	Trade Union Congress
UK	United Kingdom
US, USA	United States of America
VAT	Value Added Tax

Introduction

The Issue

Older people have been characterised by two mutually contradictory stereotypes. On the one hand they have been portrayed as a powerful lobby, growing demographically and able to demand large redistributions of the nation's income in their direction. On the other hand they have been typified as a marginalised group at high risk of poverty and exclusion and, in a political context, largely powerless. This book examines, using original research, the reality of the impact of the increasing number of older people on the British political process.

The Project

The primary purpose of this book is to present and discuss the significance of the findings of a major piece of research conducted by the Older People and Politics Project (OPPOL) within Exeter University's Sociology Department. The project had three main investigative concerns:

- How effective are pressure groups and lobbyists for older people?
- How is the power and influence of older people perceived by older people themselves and the general public?
- How are politicians responding to older people and their needs?

The project drew on a wide variety of techniques and sources to assemble data. The team researched documentary sources relating to older people's politics in general and the 1997 General Election in particular. Over a twelve-month period from May 1999 to May 2000 interviews were conducted with politicians from the three major political parties, who were identified first by their position within the party, second by their involvement with older people's issues and third by their willingness to discuss the issues. Key figures from the major charities working on behalf of older people and activists within the pensioners' movement were also interviewed. The opinions of the general public were obtained from focus groups and individual interviews held with a wide range of people. The focus groups looked at how the power and influence of older people is perceived by older people themselves and by the general public. Focus group participants were volunteers, recruited through an information stand at a city library and through contact with local organisations. The focus groups were conducted in London, a county town, and a seaside resort. The groups were also contrasted by age, gender and ethnicity. Individual interviews followed an open-ended, semi-structured schedule and lasted from 40 to 90 minutes. Interviews were taped and then transcribed and entered into the QSRNUD.IST computer program for qualitative analysis.[1] From the results obtained from the qualitative data, areas of specific interest were identified and operationalised into survey questions. The generality of perceptions derived from these interviews and focus groups was examined in a nationwide face-to-face survey of 2,087 adults aged over sixteen throughout Great Britain conducted by the polling organisation MORI.[2]

Members of the research team also observed and participated in a wide range of events and activities through which older people's interests were expressed. These included forums, public meetings, committee meetings and rallies. We attended Age Concern 'Millennium Debate of the Age' events, including the final conferences in London; the Better Government for Older People (BGOP) Learning Network Event, 25 June 1999; National Pensioners' Convention (NPC) educational weekends; National Pensioners' Convention (NPC) Full Council Meetings; a British Pensioners' Trade Union Action Association (BPTUAA) General Purpose and Finances Meeting; a Greater London Pensioners' Association Rally; a Pensioners' Rights Campaign Rally; the Greater London Forum for the Elderly's AGM; a meeting of the Hackney Pensioners' Convention; the Pensioners' Voice AGM; the Pensioners' Day March of 1999; and Pensioners' Parliament of May 2000.

Background to the Issues

Defining Old Age

Old age may be defined in many ways. Chronological age is the most obvious choice. Older adults might be thought of as being over 55, or perhaps as over 65. Alternatively, they might be defined in relation to employment, as retired people. Old age has also come to be defined

---

[1] Direct quotations from these interviews and focus groups presented in this book are referenced with the initials OPPOL.

[2] Our questions were placed on MORI's Omnibus, a nationally representative quota sample of 2,087 adults interviewed throughout Great Britain by MORI/Field & Tab across 151 constituency-based sampling points. Interviews were carried out face to face using Computer Assisted Personal Interviewing in respondents' homes between 31 March and 3 April 2000. The data have been weighted to reflect the national population profile.

through a political context. As retired people are generally entitled to receive some sort of state pension, age becomes 'a politically important characteristic since pension systems are a direct result of political decisions about how surplus wealth will be redistributed' (Quadagno and Street, 1996:378). The establishment of old age pensions systems created chronological definitions of old age based on retirement from work. Older people are simultaneously thought to be those who have retired from work and those over the legal retirement age (60 for women, 65 for men). However, these two criteria coincide less and less. Old age can also be defined by family cycle, for example through reference to grandparenthood. It might even be defined through some self-assessment of health or frailty – feeling 'old'.

Older people are not a homogeneous group; they exhibit as much diversity as the general population does. Separating off a demarcated category of 'older people' as an area of study risks marginalising them by implying they are different from and more of a problem than 'us' who are not old (Baars, 1991). The research team saw themselves as simply studying a group of adults who are older than the rest – that is to say, a comparative and situated category rather than an absolute criterion. Discovering our informants' definitions of old age was an important part of the study. The team were asked by interviewees and interested parties how *we* defined such terms.

The research team decided that they should not look to exclude people or adopt a formal definition; rather to explore the activity of election campaigning to see how people develop categories and criteria. The team tried to let respondents define the category themselves and, when pushed, we defined the discussion in term of 'retired people'. Interestingly, we had some people in our focus groups who were defined as younger people in terms of our selection criterion, i.e. under 55, but who insisted on speaking as older people because of their relative age to the rest of the group. The terms in which people speak of older people are not 'natural' categories but refer to a diversity of people with varying needs, goals, aspirations, social classes, states of health, economic and welfare conditions, life stages and other interests and characteristics. The research team tried to avoid the assumption that age groups are automatically socially relevant categories. It is highly probable that often the only characteristic that binds members of age groups together is the number of birthdays they have experienced.

Democracy and the Political Process

In seeking to understand the impact of an ageing population on the 'political process', we must determine what is meant by that term. Our research subjects had a variety of conceptualisations of the nature of the

British political process. Important to our research subjects' beliefs about the political process is the idea of democracy. Whatever their beliefs about the actuality of the political process, there was a strong normative consensus around the values of democracy. Political and social science, in order to compare and contrast a wide range of political systems, also develop definitions of democracy and types of democracies. The concept of democracy, as described by Beetham and Boyle (1995:1), 'embodies the ideal that decisions affecting an association as a whole should be taken by all its members, and that they should each have equal rights to take part in such decisions'. These authors, in simplifying their concept of democracy, say that democracy 'entails the twin principles of *popular control* of decision-making and *equality of rights* to exercise that control'. If we use this as an initial working definition, it would be anticipated that a democratic political process should reflect the needs and wants of the electorate in some proportion to the social composition of its members. It could thus be hypothesised that as society becomes older, political outcomes should change to reflect the needs and wants of an older population.

It is possible to contrast 'participatory' with 'electoral' democracy. The British Parliamentary system is seen as being based on the election of representatives who act in Parliament to choose a government and to make laws. Voting in elections is seen as the main means of democratic expression in a mass society. We can therefore seek to identify the impact of older voters in electoral outcomes. Participatory democracy sees politics as a continuous process in which citizens are included in decision making. Such participation needs mechanisms in addition to elections to incorporate citizens and articulate their interests. Thus it is also possible to examine the role of interest groups and consultation mechanisms in order to identify the impact of an increased number of older citizens. Only if there are 'effective and consistent channels of influence and pressure' from people 'does government policy reflect' people's needs (Beetham and Boyle, 1995:3).

Pensions Issues

Pensions schemes are run by three different kinds of institution. There are state-run schemes, in which the national treasury and civil service play the key administrative roles and in which people participate as citizens. There are private schemes, in which people participate as private customers of commercial (or, decreasingly, mutual) organisations that administer the schemes. There are also occupational schemes, in which people participate as employees and to which employers also make a contribution. In these cases the assets remain part of the employing institution but are frequently managed by commercial companies or special public consortia. There are two basic ways in which the finances of pensions scheme are organised; these are 'funded' schemes and 'pay as you go' (PAYG) schemes. Funded schemes have the characteristics of savings schemes, whereby the contributions are invested in a fund from which pensions are paid as contributors become entitled. Thus pensions are backed by assets, usually in the form of stock-market investments (which of course may fall as well as rise in value). PAYG schemes pay current pensions from the current contributions. They are quicker to establish than are other types of scheme and are the predominant mechanism for public pensions.

The key public policy issues with respect to pensions are:

- Security – do private or public schemes represent a more reliable way to deliver pensions in the next generation (are market failures a bigger risk than political failures in delivering promised future pensions)?
- Targeting – do means-tested pensions provide a disincentive for people to prepare for their old age and unfairly penalise those who have saved for their old age, or are they efficient means of targeting scarce resources at the most needy?
- Social solidarity – do universal pensions ensure nationwide commitment to maintaining the pension (whereas means tests create opposing interests between recipients and those paying), or do they create an unsustainable burden on the working population?

A Brief Overview of the Political Sociology of Later Life

This study was conceived as an exercise in political sociology but will draw broadly on ideas and information from the fields of social gerontology, demography, politics and social policy. The social impact of an ageing population is the subject of considerable academic interest (Midwinter and Tester, 1987; Vincent, 1995, 1999; Featherstone and Wernick, 1995; Benington, 1996). As early as 1944, the Royal Commission on Population spoke of 'the considerable political coverage' that would be required to withstand well-mobilised pensioner pressure (Midwinter and Tester, 1987). There is considerable material written on the American context. Pampel, for example, has tried to assess to what extent it is possible to discern shifts in political power that follow from demographic change and how these affect the distribution of resources managed by the state (Pampel and Williamson, 1989; Pampel, 1998). Binstock (1994, 1997) and Binstock and Day (1995) have looked at old age politics in the US. Achenbaum (1983, 1997), Pratt (1976, 1993, 1995), Haber and Gratton (1994) and others have looked at the history of the pensioners' movement in America. From a critical gerontological perspective, writers such as Estes, working alone

(1979, 1989) and with co-writers (1984a, 1984b, 1993, 1996), and Quadagno and Street (1996) have examined the politics of provision for the elderly in America. The specific impact of older people's politics in a British context have been discussed by, amongst others, Ginn and Arber (1999), Bornat (1998) and Blaikie (1990). Macnicol and Blaikie (1989) have examined the history of the pension and the pensioners' movement. Phillipson (1982, 1991, 1998) and Walker (1987, 1992a, 1992b, 1996, 1998) have made contributions to understanding the politics of old age. Walker has concentrated on age and politics in a European context (Walker and Maltby, 1997; Walker and Naegele, 1999). Walker (1998) is a good short introduction to the topic. He neatly summarises the existing knowledge and makes the case that political mobilisation among older people will increase and that local authorities will play a key role in that process.

This book discusses the politics of old age in terms of the 'pensioner's movement'. There are three possible referents for this phrase. There is a restricted meaning that limits the 'pensioners' movement' to those organisations that are run by and for pensioners. There is also a wider range of organisations including many charities and voluntary organisations that take an interest in the well-being of older people that might also be included in the 'pensioners' movement'. Finally, the term can also be used to refer to a social movement that reflects a set of values and concerns – namely improved social conditions for older people – and is manifest amongst a wide range of individuals as well as organisations. The structure of the book requires a progressively expanded use of the term as the focus moves from specific organisations to broader themes of public opinion and social change.

Book Contents by Chapter

The first two chapters of this book outline the fundamental background to the significance of an ageing population. Chapter 1 sets out the demographic background and indicates the nature and size of changes in the electorate. Chapter 2 provides further essential political context for understanding contemporary fears about an ageing population; in particular it looks at the historical development of the issue of an ageing population. The next three chapters present material on organisations that represent older people. Chapter 3 looks at pensioners' organisations run by pensioners and explores their campaigning priorities and links with trade unions. Chapter 4 explores the role of the charities – organisations acting as advocates for older people, examines their relationship with the broader pensioners' movement and discusses the limitations of campaigning within the restrictions of charitable status. Chapter 5 examines institutions and groups that provide a mechanism for older people to express their views to government. These include forums and other initiatives for facilitating public debate and getting the voice of older people heard. Chapter 6 explores the influence of older voters in the specific case of the 1997 General Election. The main features of the campaign are presented and the impact of age on the election assessed. Chapter 7 explores the influence of the pensioners' movement on the specific issue of the state pension. It presents a contemporary history of the pensions issue and seeks to identify the influence that the ageing of the population may have had. Chapter 8 looks in detail at evidence on older people and public opinion. It explores how older people are perceived in a political context and what collective responsibilities towards older people are thought to exist. The chapter also looks at how older people perceive themselves and their political power. The final chapter, 9, brings together two key themes which emerge from the book, those of citizenship and generation. Generation rather than age appears to be the feature that shapes attitudes and political opinions. Ideas of citizenship and the future of the welfare state are linked to the experience of particular generations. The Conclusion outlines the challenges for the pensioners' movement that emerge from the research findings presented throughout the book.

1 The Debate –
The Significance of an
Ageing Electorate

Introduction

The extent to which demographic change has been seen to be a problem has varied considerably over time. There seems to be an increasingly widely held belief in contemporary Britain that the ageing of the population is creating significant social problems, indeed even constitutes a crisis. It is possible to examine the evidence of demographic change and the reasons why population issues have been considered problematic throughout the twentieth century. This first chapter considers the changes that have occurred to the balance of age groups in the UK population and what impact this has had on the size and age profile of the electorate.

Numbers

In the pre-modern era in Europe and America there was chronic uncertainty about the length of life. Demographic characteristics of the time included very high rates of infant mortality, death in childbirth and epidemics of fatal infectious diseases. On the whole, living standards and nutritional levels militated against living in a healthy condition to a ripe old age. One of the successes of modern society has been to improve health and increase life expectancy. People are now much more likely to live a full life span and die in their 80s. Current British life expectancy at birth is approximately 74 years for men and 80 years for women. The life expectancy difference is somewhat less at age 60, at which age men can anticipate an average further eighteen years of life to age 78, while women can typically expect to live a further twenty-two years to age 82 (Jackson, 1998).

It has been argued that the typical age of death is becoming more standard. Although average longevity is increasing, there is a debate as to whether there is a naturally set maximum available life span that is being reached by greater numbers of people (Victor, 1991; Gilleard and Higgs,

1998). Some see death as a technical problem solvable by science and technology; others see the quest for the indefinite postponement of death as merely the perpetuation of a centuries-old fantasy fuelled by fear. The largest gains in life expectancy have been the result of a dramatic fall in infant mortality and not, as popularly believed, of an increased life expectancy for the old. In practice, the twentieth century increase in the average life span has had more to do with keeping babies and children alive than it has with postponing death for 90-year-olds. Improvements in sanitation, housing and nutrition; vaccinations and the miracle of antibiotics; as well as numerous other social and medical breakthroughs mean that now more than ever before most of us have a good chance of reaching old age.

There are three key components to the ageing of modern populations, the most important being increased life expectancy at birth. The second is the decline in fertility, which means that younger cohorts are smaller than those which have gone before. The third is the recent development of increased life expectancy in old age; however, this remains a small component of the overall global trend. The increase in life expectancy combined with the advent of contraception and modern ideas about family size means that the British population has been ageing for most of the twentieth century and is expected to continue to do so until the middle of the twenty-first century. In 1998 the Department of Social Security (DSS, 1998:1) estimated that by 2031, 41% of the UK's population will be over 50, 23% over retirement age and 6% over 80.

In 1851, when the UK population was recorded as 20.8 million, there were only 1.3 million people of 'pensionable age' (6.1% of the population). The percentage of elderly people in the population remained static at around 6.2% until the census of 1911, by which time the population of the country as a whole had doubled to 40.8 million. It was around this time that the proportion of the population in the pensionable age range started to grow significantly. The annual increase in the population counted as elderly grew from 1.1% to nearly 2%. The acceleration in the numbers of pensionable-age people in Britain reached its peak in 1931, when the census showed that the population was 44.8 million, of whom 4.3 million were of pensionable age (9.6% of the population). The number of pensioners in the population was at this time increasing by 2.5% per year; subsequently this rate of growth declined. An important transition in population structure was recorded in the 1971 census, which revealed that the *rate* at which the proportion of older people in the population was expanding ceased to grow. Although the absolute numbers of pensioners continued to grow, the average annual increase in the numbers of pensioners started to fall. The 1981 census found that there were 54.3 million people in Great Britain, 9.6 million of whom were of pensionable age, and this represented 17.7% of the population as a whole. However, the average annual increase in numbers of pensioners had declined to less than 1% (cf. Chart 1.1).

Census forecasts by the Office of National Statistics for the United Kingdom (1998) suggest that the number of pensioners will have risen from 10.668 million in 1996 to 11.956 million in 2021, with 5.36 million aged over 75. However, these numbers are affected by the raising of the

Chart 1.1 Size of UK age groups 1891, 1951, 1991 and 2051

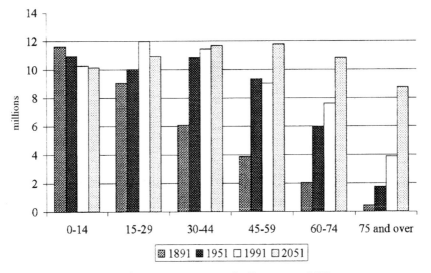

Source: OPCS, 1993, and the Government Actuaries Department, 2000.

pension age for women; had it remained static at 60, the total population of pensionable-age people in 2021 would have been projected as 14.0 million. At the same time, the working population will increase from 36.035 million in 1996 to 39.229 million in 2021. This means that if the ages from which the state pension is paid are not changed again, the ratio between the numbers of people 'of working age' to the numbers of people over retirement age will fall from 3.38:1 in 1996 to 3.28:1 in 2021.

Chart 1.2 UK population projections indexed on 1995

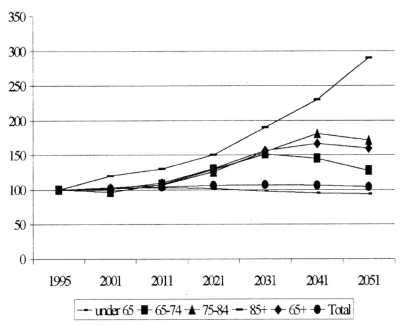

Note: Each data series is set to a value of 100 in the start year (1995) and changes in later years are measured in proportion to the start year.
Source: Royal Commission on Long-term Care, March 1999.

The proportion of the very elderly, those people over 75 years of age, in British society will continue to rise. This pattern of growth in the very elderly population can be illustrated by Office of Population Census and Surveys (OPCS, 1993) population projections based on the results of the 1991 census. The total population will grow, in their estimation, by 7.8%, from 57.6 million to 62.1 million, by the year 2031. The numbers over retirement age projected for 2031 will have grown by 51.8% (approximately 1.3% per annum). Between 1991 and 2031 the numbers over 75 years in age are projected to grow by 70% (cf. Chart 1.2).

The demographic position for the UK is that its population will age less quickly and to a lesser extent during the first forty years of the twenty-first century than will the populations of much of the rest of the world and indeed of Europe. This is because, as a nation, the UK went through the 'demographic transition' earlier and at a slower rate than many other countries. The number of people aged 65 and over per hundred people aged 15-65 in Europe stood at 15.1 in 1960 but is expected to rise to 29.1 by

2025. In Britain the equivalent figure will change from 17.9 in 1960 to a predicted 29.7 in 2025. This changing ratio is a feature of all industrialised countries. It is most significantly a feature of those societies whose birth rates declined rapidly in the 1950s and 1960s (Hills, 1993). In Europe, while Sweden has a relatively old population at the present time, countries like Italy, whose fertility rate has transformed much more rapidly, will in the first part of the next century see their populations ageing even more dramatically. Ireland, Portugal and Greece, with relatively high proportions

Table 1.1   Ageing populations in European countries

Country	% of pop. aged 60 and over, 1993	% of pop. aged 60 and over, 2020	Increase
Sweden	22.4	26.3	3.9
Denmark	20.1	24.3	4.2
UK	20.6	25.3	4.7
Portugal	19.5	25.5	6.0
Ireland	15.3	21.8	6.5
Greece	20.8	27.3	6.5
Austria	19.8	26.5	6.7
Luxembourg	19.2	26.3	7.1
Netherlands	17.6	24.8	7.2
Germany	20.4	27.7	7.3
Spain	19.6	27.2	7.6
Belgium	21.1	28.8	7.7
France	18.7	26.7	8.0
Italy	21.3	29.9	8.6
Finland	18.8	28.2	9.4

Source: Modified from Walker and Maltby (1997:10).

of rural population and a strong religious stance against birth control, show signs of following a similar route of declining fertility rates followed by an ageing population but are doing so somewhat later than the rest of the EC.

Changes in the Electorate

While changes in the age structure of the electorate in the UK follow the demographic trends outlined above, they have also been significantly affected by electoral reform and changes in the law. The following charts use the census records of population modified by the changes in law to estimate the changing age structure of the population entitled to vote.

Historically Britain has not had a 'one person, one vote' electoral system. There were a variety of entitlements to vote derived from property, business and university rights, gender and age. The changes in entitlement to vote came with the Reform Acts, particularly in 1884 with expanded male suffrage for those over 21 years of age who met property qualifications. Alderman (1978) suggests that about 60% of adult males had the vote as a result of this Act. In the twentieth century, women over the age of 29 were given the right to vote in 1918 and in the same

Chart 1.3 Numbers of voters and older voters 1891-1991

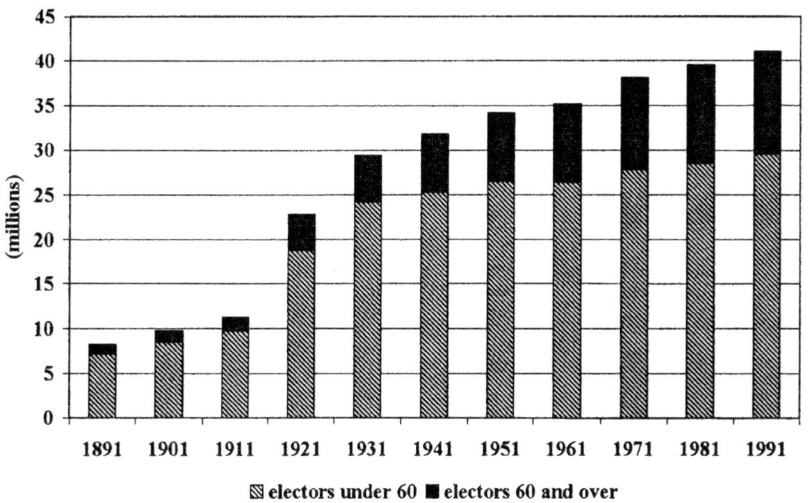

Source: Calculated from OPCS Census Report: Historical Data 1991.

legislation the property qualification was removed. In 1929 the voting age for men and women was equalised. In 1969 the voting age was lowered from 21 to 18. These age-based changes are incorporated in Charts 1.3 and 1.4. However, until 1949, multiple voting, whereby some individuals had additional votes, was also common. People with property or other special franchise rights made up the business vote and the university vote. Morris (1969) estimates that in 1910 these multiple votes might have amounted to as many as half a million. Changes in the franchise over the last three decades have included extensions to voluntary patients in mental health institutions and some overseas residents. As there is no method of estimating the age of those with multiple votes or those excluded by property qualifications, we have not attempted to include them in the data. Chart 1.3 refers to the size of the population entitled to vote by age at each census and indicates the numbers aged 60 or over. Chart 1.4 shows the proportion of the electorate in that age category.

Because there are more older women than older men, and because women under 30 were not enfranchised, the 1918 changes not only greatly expanded the electorate but also significantly raised the average age of voters. However, the basic demographic trend is clear in the age profile of the electorate. Over the century ageing accelerated in the first half and tapered off in the second. Although the absolute numbers of older voters, and in particular very old voters, continue to increase, the rate of change has slowed. The proportion of voters over retirement age will also be diminished by the raising of the retirement age for women to 65, which comes into effect in 2010. Therefore, demographically speaking, the

Chart 1.4 Percentage of electorate aged 60 and over 1891-1991

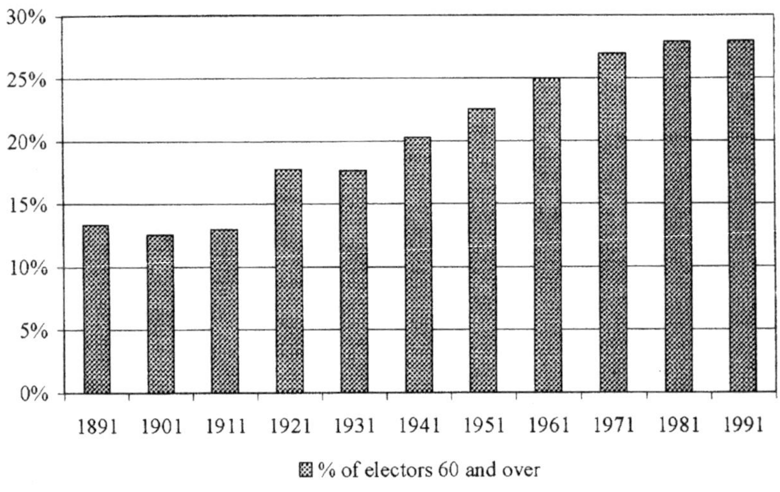

☒ % of electors 60 and over

Source: Calculated from OPCS Census Report: Historical Data 1991.

increasing proportion of older voters is not something new. The proportion of people over 65 has been increasing since the first decade of the twentieth century. Although the absolute numbers are now larger, the rate at which this proportion grew peaked in the 1930s.

Why does it appear, if the demography has been changing for at least eighty years, that only now is the electoral power of older voters being considered an issue? The demographic change has significance for electoral politics only to the extent to which age groups manifest common political behaviour, and the extent to which political elites identify age-based categories of voters as having electoral significance. It is important to distinguish between the actual impact of the numbers of older electors and beliefs about this impact. There are changes occurring as politicians and older people respond to media hype about the so-called 'demographic timebomb' and the potential importance of the 'grey vote'. However, these are effects of ideologies and belief systems and not of the actual numbers themselves. Further, it is important to distinguish between the concerns *of* older people and concerns *about* older people, between the agenda of older voters and older people as the subjects of other people's political agendas.

What sources of evidence can lead to a proper grasp of the contemporary political realities? What contemporary evidence can we find on the power or lack of power of older people that can provide a critical commentary on the different ideological positions and the rhetoric of the 'problem of old age'? We can direct our attention to three questions and seek empirical data with which to comment on those questions. To what extent are older people identified, by themselves and others, as a coherent political interest group with a distinctive agenda? To what extent do older people form organisations capable of articulating a clear set of demands and campaigning effectively on these? How responsive is the political system in general and the political elite – in particular senior party figures and officials – to the needs and demands of older people? These questions form the basis of the studies we report in the following chapters.

2 The Nature of Fears About an Ageing Population

Introduction

In 1970, a visiting professor at the University of California, San Diego, got very impatient at the conservative retirees flocking into Southern California and trying to impose their values, with Governor Ronald Reagan's help, upon the University of California's emancipated students. So impatient was he that he published in *The New Republic* an article charmingly entitled "Disfranchise the Old." Here is its trenchant conclusion:

'There are simply too many senile voters and their number is growing. The vote should not be a privilege in perpetuity, guaranteed by minimal physical survival, but a share in the continuing fate of the political community, both in its benefits and its risks. The old, having no future, are dangerously free from the consequences of their own political acts, and it makes no sense to allow the vote to someone who is actuarially unlikely to survive, and pay the bills for, the politician or party he [sic] may help elect...I would advocate that all persons lose the vote at retirement or age 70, whichever is earlier.' (Douglas J. Stewart, "Disfranchise the Old," *New Republic* 29(8):20-22)

One generation later, the concern that the elderly are becoming politically too powerful has taken on, in a number of countries, unprecedented proportions. The main fear is no longer that the elderly may be animated "by a desire to see old prejudices vindicated" (ibid.), that they may use their electoral strength to impose their values. It is rather that they may use it in an excessive manner to benefit their unavoidably short-term self-interests. (Phillipe Van Parijs, 1999)

This chapter examines who it is that identifies older people as a social problem, and explores the basis of the social construction of older people as a potentially influential force in politics. Many commentators see older people as becoming a significant political force, although fewer see them as a currently powerful lobby.

There are some advocates raising the prospect of older people using the ballot box to force politicians to address their issues (Midwinter,

1991). This quotation illustrates the kind of rhetoric used by many activists in the pensioners' movement:

> PENSIONER POWER! The population is getting older – with 30% of us now over 50 – and our politicians are now starting to wake up to the idea that the voice of the older generation will be ignored at their peril! (Chris White, *Golden Age*, October 1987)

Those people advocating the rights of older people have a clear interest in maximising the political leverage that increased numbers might bring. There are others who raise warnings about the threat of militant pensioners to governmental fiscal propriety (Preston, 1984; Thurow, 1996; World Bank, 1994). From the mid-1980s concerns were expressed about 'generational equity'. This is the idea that older people of the current generation are obtaining benefits at the expense of younger generations. Sometimes this is expressed as older people receiving state benefits at the expense of children. More frequently it is expressed as the current generation obtaining from state pension schemes more than they contributed, while succeeding generations will get less. Although the nature of the problem and possible solutions are keenly contested political issues, in the 1990s in Britain and the US it has become a commonplace notion that society is facing a crisis over an ageing population. The radical right that came to political prominence in the 1980s and 1990s are part of the free market tradition. Their response to older people, whom they see as taking an increasing portion of welfare, is framed by this tradition. Their preferred solutions to social reform are potentially blocked by older people as an interest group using their numbers to preserve the role of the state in welfare provision (Walker, 1987, 1996). To these people, organised older citizens are potentially a dangerous pressure group.

Historical Development of the Issue of an Ageing Population

Media discussion suggests that demographic change as an issue is a recent phenomenon. However, neither the demographic ageing of the population nor the identification of this change as an issue is new. Indeed, demography from its origins has been driven by perceived social problems. Malthus (1970) writing in the late eighteenth century was responding to an unprecedented growth in the British population when he wrote about the inevitability of unchecked population growth outstripping production, and famine, disease and calamity checking population growth if humans did not curb their passions. Katz (1996:69) argues that 'alarmist demography and gerontological knowledge came together in the social surveys of the late nineteenth and early twentieth centuries that decried the growth rate and poverty of the elderly population as an economic and moral crisis'. In the period following the acceptance of Darwinian theories of evolution and the First World War, the eugenics movement was concerned about changing patterns of fertility. They argued that the intelligent and educated were having fewer children than the poor and ignorant were and this would lower the intelligence and genetic potential of the nation (Overbeek, 1974, 1977).

Between the two world wars the population ceased to grow. Concerns were raised at the time that this would create problems in the supply and flexibility of labour. It was suggested that a growing population would stimulate demand. During the Second World War the fertility rate of British women fell to what was then an all-time low. These problems were thought serious enough to have a Royal Commission on the Population, which reported in 1949. Although the issue the Commission were appointed to look at came to be seen as less immediate with the postwar baby boom, they nevertheless recommended a strong pro-natalist programme of family allowances, family support services and better housing directed towards encouraging increased family size. This Royal Commission also considered the issue of the ageing population, which was concomitant with the falling birth rate. They expressed concerns about the increasing average age of the labour force. They felt that the reduced number of younger workers would reduce the flexibility and adaptability of the workforce, and expressed concerns about military manpower. They commented: 'It is possible that with a diminishing proportion of young people the community might lose something in energy, initiative, enterprise and other qualities associated with youth' (Royal Commission, 1949:225).

As long as there has been a national pension system there have been concerns about its affordability. There have been a number of histories of pensions and the pensioners' movement (Macnicol and Blaikie, 1989; Blaikie, 1990; Macnicol, 1998). These studies indicate that one of the key issues influencing leading figures in government who made the decisions over the introduction and expansion of the state pension in the inter-war years was the extent to which the existing workforce could or should pay for the pensions of those who had retired. After the war, demographic concerns about the pension system were raised. Significantly, the Royal Commission said: 'with increasing numbers of the old and consequently their increasing strength as a political pressure group, it is very important that the implications of proposals for increased pensions should be realised.' (Royal Commission, 1949:224) – a sentiment that could have come directly out of a 1990s New Right tract produced fifty years later to warn of the imminent dire consequences if the state pension were not reined in. However, the major solutions proposed by the Royal Commission were not to curtail the pension and other rights of older people but to emphasise the need as they saw it to encourage families and halt the decline in the birth rate.

In the early fifties, with the welfare state established, there was continuing recognition that the ageing of the population was a potential issue. However, this period also saw unrivalled economic expansion and growth in prosperity in the West. In all major industrial democracies, but to differing extents, there was a basic consensus which recognised that the state should ensure that older people and other vulnerable groups also benefit from the increased prosperity. In Britain the welfare state was supported by all political parties, and this 'Butskilite'[3] consensus enabled growth in the economy to fund improved pensions, and health and welfare benefits. The Conservative Party's response to the growing proportion of older people is reflected in their 1955 General Election manifesto, which, although couched in partisan terms, reflects the consensus of the times.

> The nation has assumed very large obligations towards the pensioners of tomorrow; and tomorrow there will be very many more pensioners. For every 10 people of working age there are now 2 of pensionable age; but within a quarter of a century there will be 3. If during this period Britain can increase her national wealth and resources, by the policy of investment and enterprise which we advocate, these obligations can be met. But if wealth is dissipated, enterprise hampered and severe inflation brought about again by Socialist short-sightedness, the whole of our National Insurance scheme would be undermined and ultimately destroyed.
>
> In its first year of office the Conservative Government increased virtually all social service payments. This year it has again raised pensions and benefits, and fully restored the purchasing power that Parliament intended they should have when the main rates were fixed after the war. Insurance pensioners, war pensioners and public service pensioners can be sure that a Conservative Government will continue to give the most constant attention to their interests and needs.
>
> It is our wish to avoid any change in the present minimum pension ages. But these ages do not necessarily represent the limit of working life. With the aid of its National Advisory Committee the Government will continue to encourage the employment, without regard to age, of all who can give effective service and wish to do so. (Conservative Party, 1955)

Leaders in British social research and social policy have for over a century been heavily involved with older people's issues as a by-product of

---

[3] An adjective derived by mixing the names of key Conservative and Labour politicians of the day – Hugh Gaitskell and Rab Butler.

their concerns about poverty. For example, Charles Booth (1840-1916), pioneer of social surveys, and Beatrice Webb (1858-1943), a leading figure in the Fabian Society, played a role in the early pensioners' movement. Socially motivated research and campaigns for reform played a significant part in the development of the state pension. In the midst of the growing prosperity of the 1950s and '60s, social researchers such as Peter Townsend rediscovered poverty. Townsend's research on older people (Townsend, 1957; Townsend and Wedderburn, 1965) follows in the tradition of earlier social research in documenting the plight of older people in contrast to the dominant 'you've never had it so good' rhetoric of the period. Economic growth focused debate in Britain on how wealth should be shared rather than on the affordability of the welfare state. Demographic concerns in the 1960s were not directed at home to the number of elderly people, but rather overseas to population growth in the developing world and the number of babies being born.

The long postwar boom did not last. Economic growth faltered, particularly in the seventies, following the shock to the global economy of oil price rises. Recession became widespread and deep, and most developed Western democracies experienced a de-industrialisation. There was a loss of confidence that economic growth would provide a route to improved social welfare. Jack Parsons (1977) used the following quotes while demolishing 'the burden of dependency argument: the fallacy of the aging population' to illustrate some attitudes of the time.

> If we do not have a least one young worker to replace every one that retires, the old become an impossible burden on the community. (D.E.C. Eversley, from 'Is Britain being threatened by overpopulation' *Listener*, 27 July 1967)

> We have what is quite likely the heaviest burden of old-age dependency in the world. If we are to carry it without imposing an impossible task on those who do the work we shall need all the children parents are prepared to have. (Sir John Walley, letter to the *Guardian*, 24 January 1968)

> A reduction in the number of children…would mean that by the year 2001 we would have an aged dependent population of … over 7 million that we are unable to support. (Dr P.H. Millard, letter in the *Lancet*, 17 April 1971)

By the 1980s the welfare consensus of the fifties and sixties had clearly gone. The politics of the New Right with its free market solutions to social problems was the dominant force in policy development. The solutions for economic stagnation were privatisation and the enterprise culture. The idea was to 'roll back the state'. The role of state, not only in the economy but also in welfare, was queried. The New Right championed the idea of individual responsibility in making provision for old age and other life contingencies. If the economy was to be freed from the burden of the socialist state, the expensive cost of pensions and medical support would have to be reduced. The idea that demographic change could reinforce the demands for a redistributive role for the state was viewed with alarm. Two academic publications were particularly significant in raising the issue of generational equity. The demographer Samuel Preston received widespread interest from a paper published in the popular science magazine *Scientific American* (Preston, 1984). In this paper he sought to demonstrate that poor American children were losing out to older people in terms of state support. Johnson et al.'s edited volume, *Workers versus Pensioners*, published in 1989, brought this issue of generational equity to the fore in the UK.

This position on demographic change came to dominate official policy, a development clearly symbolised by World Bank publications that claimed to establish the nature of the problem and recommended policies, notably state fiscal and welfare policies, to deal with it (World Bank, 1994). Thus in the 1990s in Britain and the US it became taken for granted that society is facing a crisis over an ageing population. The nature of the problem and possible solutions are keenly contested political issues. In continental Europe, there are similar concerns. Some European countries have more rapidly ageing populations than the UK or the US and most have more generous pension systems. Many of these European pension schemes are run on the 'pay as you go' principle, that is to say, they depend on current contributions to pay the pensions of those already retired. The consequence has been a concern to promote social cohesion. When the European Union (EU) designated a special year for older people, it entitled it 'The European Year of Older People and Solidarity Between Generations'.

Thus it is possible to trace throughout the course of the twentieth century two very general approaches. One emphasises the social condition of older people based on a tradition of social research and on collectivist premises about the social responsibility of the whole community for its poorer and less powerful members. The second is rooted in the free market philosophy and is based on individualistic assumptions about personal responsibility, drawing its intellectual rigour from numerical economic and demographic analysis. These traditions have responded in various ways throughout the century to changing demographic and economic circumstances.

The radical right question the relevance of the 'deserving poor' image of older people in the contemporary world and emphasise the virtues of free-trade. They wish to roll back the state and create new markets in place of public provision. They favour individual solutions, including funded private pensions, and no redistributive role for the state. The idea of the rational self-interested individual lies at the heart of this tradition and leads such analysts to feel that older people will use their votes to protect their interests. Thus, their preferred solutions to social welfare reform could potentially be blocked by older people as an interest group using their numbers to preserve the role of the state. It is from people writing within the radical free market perspective that warnings about the danger from organised older citizens originate.

Those who have engaged in direct social research, documenting the lives of older people through the century, are under no illusions about the exclusion of their subjects from wealth, power and influence. These observers of social exclusion see older people as marginalised by the political process. Thus the most vulnerable sections of society, for example, older women, minorities, or manual workers, those who are the most dependent on state resources, fall further and further behind the rest of society and lack the power to challenge this situation effectively. Those writing from within this tradition envision collective solutions for the condition of older people. They therefore advocate strengthening social solidarity as the way forward.

These contrasting views of the 'problem of old age' tend to coincide with contrasting views of politics. On the one side there is a tradition that has its intellectual root in the liberal democratic tradition of political thought and starts with the individual citizen. This view emphasises the individual participant in the political process and sees individuals essentially as self-interested rational actors trying to maximise benefits for themselves. This is most highly developed in the ideology of the free market, in this case the political market represented by choice between political parties expressed by national ballot. From this perspective the problematic nature of demographic change lies in Tocqueville's (1835) concern with the tyranny of the majority, in particular the ability of numerically superior interest groups, including those based on age, to use their control of the state to redistribute resources in their favour.

An alternative perspective on politics starts with the state and sees it as an institution that serves the interests of the various elites that control it or can influence it. The political system may not in practice give to all sections of the community equal opportunities to have political influence and power. Thus writers taking a critical perspective suggest that the state may not be responsive to older people as a social group. Older people's lack of power may stem from a variety of factors. Older people may be socially divided and there may be no single or unified response from them towards the political system. Further, older people may experience, because of their age or generation, particular difficulties in organising and representing their interests. The consequences of this lack of power and exclusion from the political process are poverty and alienation.

The Demographic Time Bomb

Some commentators have highlighted concerns that an ageing population will result in very large increases in public expenditure on pensions and healthcare. Some of the rhetoric with which these concerns are expressed generate a sense of crisis and take on doom-laden proportions. Ginn and Arber give examples of this 'apocalyptic demography':

> Media reports have raised alarm about a grey 'timebomb' or a 'rising tide' of older people, frequently referring to older people as a 'burden' on society. An academic version warns of 'a large, growing and possibly unsustainable fiscal burden on the productive populations in developed nations' (Johnson et al. 1989:9), while the World Bank Report (1994:iii) predicts 'a looming old age crisis'. (Ginn and Arber, 1999:158)

British commentary tends to be more polite and less vituperative than the US debate. However, apocalyptic demography is clearly represented in political discourse. Newspapers carry headlines such as 'Grey timebomb at the heart of the Western welfare state' (Ian Traynor, *Guardian*, 27 January 1996), or 'Wrinklies timebomb waiting to explode' (*Sunday Times*, 23 February 1997). Politicians also make reference to this view of pensioners. Michael Heseltine, the then deputy leader of the Conservative Party, said in a televised BBC election debate immediately prior to the 1997 General Election:

> Now, we're the only party that has addressed this fundamental issue of an ageing population but everybody recognised that it was the Tories that were looking ahead with radical ideas in Social Security, in Pensions,...And that leaves a gap between those who only have the State Pension. Now the taxpayer can't afford to increase the State Pension to match what's happening in the private sector – everyone knows that – overnight. But we've looked ahead to this generation and we've said that we will start – probably in about four years' time – we will start to create for everybody their own investment scheme which will be funded every year by contributions based on their National Insurance scheme. (BBC Transcript)

In government, Labour have denied that there was a pensions timebomb but have nevertheless effectively continued the policy of limiting future state liabilities for pensions. Gisella Stuart, a then newly appointed junior minister at the Department of Health, speaking at the Millennium Debate of the Age (6 December 1999) commenced her speech by pointing out that the government had given Age Concern financial backing and a lead role in the International Year of Older People. This was followed by a statement that she did not accept the 'demographic timebomb' scenario, but she then qualified this by suggesting there were issues to be addressed as the result of demographic change – in particular, physical frailty and financial support. A Liberal Democrat spokesperson pointed out by citing dubious demography how pension provision is now made more complicated:

> I was at a seminar recently and one of the speakers said that he was convinced that average life expectancy would be 120 very shortly. And if that is the situation then clearly the whole thinking about how we deal with the pensions issue would have to go to a whole different level. All the present thinking about funded pensions and how they work is clearly not going to keep people decently till they are 120. (OPPOL interview)

Discussions concerning welfare benefits present younger people and older people as being in competition for limited welfare resources. Young families are increasingly more likely to be considered worthy recipients of these resources. A *Times* article reported results from the Family Resource Survey (1996) which showed that 'parents with young, dependent children were generally less well off than other couples' (Frean, 1999:6). This view was mirrored by former Conservative minister Peter Bottomley:

> Forty years ago, 1949, when would people have been at their poorest? The answer is when they retired. Virtually nobody had a full state-funded pension; even that was pretty low. What proportion of people are owning their own homes or have paid off their own homes by the time they retire? The answer is 80%. So nowadays when people are at their poorest is when they have the first child, going from two incomes and two mouths to feed to one income and three mouths to feed. If you or I have an elderly person in our household, say an 80-year-old father, the minimum income the state will give is about £100 a week, even though they are living with us. If you are a child, an active teenager, aged 15, the maximum they'll give is £15. Who costs more? An 80-year-old or a 15-year-old? The answer is that 15-year-olds cost several times more. I'm not saying every pensioner is well off. That's not true, but most people anywhere from 60 to 90 are much better off. (Peter Bottomley, Conservative MP, OPPOL interview)

The point here is not to question Bottomley's genuine point about the disadvantages experienced by younger people, but rather to illustrate how the issue becomes constructed as one in which the 'old' are pitched against the 'young'.

The elderly have become the scapegoats for a failing social security system. The merits of the 'demographic timebomb' case are dubious and ideologically fuelled (Vincent, 1996; Mullan, 2000). It has been shown in a number of studies that the continuation of current levels of growth in productivity in the economy will generate more than enough resources to meet existing pension commitments (see for example Johnson and Falkingham, 1992; Hills, 1993, 1996; Mullan, 2000). Fear of the demographic timebomb has generated a number of responses to the question of the future of pensions and health funding. One response is to question the priorities of government expenditure – 'commentators argue that the issue is less one of fiscal crisis than of the distribution of public expenditure between competing priorities' (Benington, 1998:7). Should money be diverted from other government expenditure to meet the presumed shortfall in pension contributions? Bruce Kent, for example, made this point by comparing Britain's high *per capita* expenditure on arms and defence and the comparatively low figure on pensions. A second and radically different response is to question whether there is a role for government in the provision of retirement incomes at all.

Debates Over the Role of Government

At the centre of any discussion about politics and old age, there is a growing debate about the proper role of the state in providing income security and healthcare for its citizens. Quadagno and Street (1996:387), for example, refer back to Marshal (1964) to point out the significance of citizenship to welfare:

> The development of Social Security in the capitalist democracies has been inextricably linked to the development of citizenship – rights and entitlements that attach to persons by virtue of their membership in a national community rather than to their property, status or market capacity.

Fears of the impending demographic situation, which promises high percentages of older citizens who will not be supported by paid employment, have led politicians to consider handing over the responsibilities of pensions and healthcare for older people to the individuals themselves. This is presented as a practical necessity, although, of course, changing the balance between public and private provision does nothing to alter the availability of active workers and resources to sustain older people in the future. Many on the New Right argue that state provision is inefficient and could be arranged more effectively through the market. Others raise the issue as a moral question: Should older people's welfare needs be a priority, or should the state avoid a role in compulsory redistribution resources from one section of the population to another? The central political issue is about what type of society we want to live in. This was made explicit in an interview with a spokesperson for the Liberal Democrats, who said:

> Is the existence of the National Health Service a token of a society in which people share each other's burdens, or are we a society where people pay for everything – individuals just pay for themselves? We have to do something about the people at the bottom who can't do it for themselves. (OPPOL interview)

Concerns about an ageing population are encouraging people to rethink the role of the state, and many believe that their role should now focus more on those in need rather than providing retirement income for the whole population.

> Traditionally we have had state-provided pensions which are the main source of income for a lot of people. But people have been expected to live not that long. We're now moving to a period where people will be living a long time in retirement and possibly have a considerable period of needing a lot of support and – I'm not accepting this point of view – but there is a point of view that what the state should do is actually get out of pension provision, and say to people that they have got to have their own pension provision, but put a lot of money into social care because that is more difficult for people. I mean everybody is going to get old, everybody is going to retire and therefore everybody should able to predict that they need money put aside for their retirement. (A Liberal Democrat party official, OPPOL interview)

Older People as a Powerful Self-Interested Political Force

Because their sheer numbers will make them a potentially powerful political force, will older people be able to ensure that resources are redistributed to them? An initial consideration of voting behaviour might make this seem a likely scenario. Respected lobbyists think it possible. Sally Greengross,[4] Director General of Age Concern, said: 'Twenty-four

---

[4] Sally Greengross subsequently retired as Director General in 2000 and was succeeded by Gordon Lishman.

percent of the electorate is over state pension age and 58% of the electorate is over forty. Almost 50% of the electorate is over 45' (OPPOL interview). The increasing numbers of older voters mean that they potentially have the ability to vote as a block and therefore influence election outcomes. However, in order for older people to mobilise in such a way, they must both identify with and be prepared to vote on age related issues. Ward (1993) identifies a qualified 'aging group consciousness' in an American context, but there are striking differences between British and US old-age politics. As Gail Wilson (2000:47) says, 'We have to ask whether older people will bother to vote, whether they will vote as a block and how will they balance the wider interests of their community or country as against their own sectional interests?'.

Surveys done on the issues that people say matter most when deciding how to vote appear to illustrate that age-related issues are taken seriously. People aged over 65 are most likely to consider pensions and care for the elderly important, whereas people aged 17 to 24 are most concerned with education and employment (British Election Survey, 1997). Fifty-seven percent of people surveyed in the Anchor Survey of July-August 1996 said that 'they would be more likely to vote for a party which pledged increased financial support for long term care and more local services for older people' (Bornat, 1998:195). Wilson (2000) suggests that political parties will begin to take note of older voters, especially where there is the potential to unite on a single issue. However, in reality, voting behaviour is rarely based on a single issue, but rather takes in a whole gambit of issues and factors, such as party allegiance and peer and parental influence. The empirical issue of how older people vote is examined in detail in Chapter 6.

The key to understanding the current socially constructed images of older people either as a dangerous pressure group or a marginalised minority lies in political philosophy. Mullan (2000) cogently argues that it is the New Right critique of the welfare role of the state rather than the demographic facts that lies behind the raising of the spectre of the 'timebomb'. The dilemmas of the modern nation state – what role government should have, what influence individual states can have on economic affairs in a globalised world economy – impact on older people. The solutions to these dilemmas are political. There are at least two sides to every political conflict. Asking who is questioning the role that the state should play in the provision of pensions and in redistributing national wealth is the starting point for understanding older people's politics as an empirical reality. It helps us understand who the protagonists are.

3   Representing Older People –
Pensioners' Organisations

Introduction

How do older people organise themselves politically? How do they campaign nationally and with what impact? This chapter examines these issues by limiting our view of the pensioners' movement to strictly those organisations of senior citizens themselves as opposed to the broader social movement of all those who seek improvements in the social condition of older people.

Organisations of Pensioners

The pensioners' movement has been active for the whole of the twentieth century. It has, however, not formed part of the dominant narrative of British social history:

> In narrative terms the Pensioners' Movement has largely been invisible and with few exceptions, scarcely any written or recorded history has been attempted. With few exceptions (Goodman, 1987; Blaikie, 1990; Miles, 1994) this has been a neglected topic by both older and younger historians, gerontologists and policy makers. (Bornat, 1998:184)

The pensioners' movement has changed to reflect the differing social and economic circumstances of the periods in which it has operated. It has periodically influenced and been influenced by the politics and social policies of the times. It clearly played an important part in the establishment of a national pension scheme and its enhancement in the first three decades of the twentieth century. It can be said to have had a major influence in the founding of the welfare state, particularly through powerful campaigns immediately prior to the Second World War. The foundations of the welfare state were laid with the 1942 Beveridge Report on 'Social Insurance and Allied Services'. It formed the basis of legislation that consolidated the responsibility for pensions and health insurance with the state, and part of the impetus for commissioning the report came from pressure from pensioners' representatives. 'The principle of state social insurance was accepted by most trade unions and employers' (Ginn and Arber, 1999:153). Yet pensioners' organisations were critical of some aspects of the report. The leadership of the National Federation of Old Age Pensions Associations clearly thought of Beveridge as representing middle class interests against those of working people. They disliked, for example, the requirement to cease work to be eligible for an insurance-based pension (Macnicol, 2000). There is a direct continuity between the pensioners' organisations that campaigned for the establishment of the state pension in the early years of the twentieth century, those that campaigned for its enhancement and extended benefits and coverage through the middle years, and those that at the end of the twentieth century are campaigning for the maintenance and retention of the state pension.

In 1999-2000, while our research was conducted, the main pensioners' organisations were Pensioners' Voice, the British Pensioners' Trade Union Action Association (BPTUAA) and the National Pensioners' Convention (NPC). Their relationship to the trade union movement and political parties from postwar to present day is an important background to understanding their current attitudes and activities. It is these and a number of smaller and more local organisations that constitute the narrowly defined pensioners' movement considered in this chapter.

National Federation of Old Age Pensions Associations (NFOAPA)

The National Federation of Old Age Pensions Associations was one of the earliest organisations to campaign for a higher state pension. Founded in 1938, it is now known as Pensioners' Voice and has over 350 branches and some 25,000 members. It operates through thirteen regions, with seven area councils and has three regional councils. 'Officers of the organisation meet regularly with government ministers and with the All Party Parliamentary Group for Pensioners, although evidence of any positive influence through this route is lacking' (Ginn and Arber, 1999:161). One informed source described the NFOAPA as originally a movement of 'what you might call "concerned citizens" – people who were likely to be magistrates or local councillors who were getting very concerned at the poverty of their older family members or constituents'.

Like pensioners' organisations of today, the NFOAPA saw itself as representing working-class interests. The NFOAPA's main tactic was to petition Parliament. In 1940 it presented a petition to Parliament that was signed by two million people. As a direct result of its petition, the NFOAPA was invited to participate in the deliberations of the Beveridge Committee. The Committee's report, published in 1942, is seen by many as the foundation of the modern welfare state. However, the NFOAPA was profoundly suspicious of the Committee and rejected its findings (Bornat,

1998; Blaikie, 1990). Such an uncompromising attitude is in keeping with the radicalism of the movement, which has consistently placed itself in opposition to government initiatives and resisted moves to co-opt pensioners by means of offering them a place at the table.

In 1944 the wartime Coalition Government's White Paper recommended an increase in pensions, which the Labour government implemented in 1946, having consulted with the NFOAPA. This change came a full two years ahead of the National Insurance Bill that became law in 1948. That an organisation which ten years before had consisted of half a dozen men meeting in a Manchester Railway waiting room should have wrested from the then minister for pensions, James Griffiths, such a concession is a testimony to the success of the pensioners' movement, and a source of pride to the current Pensioners' Voice membership. However, the pensioners' movement was, after gaining considerably in its reputation and numbers in the early 1940s, gradually to lose momentum. That loss of organisational momentum can be related to the fact that although conditions in postwar Britain were extremely austere for older people by today's standards, they contrasted with the poverty of the 1930s and reflected a greater sense of optimism for future prosperity and social justice.

Bornat (1998:185) suggests that the initial success of the pensioners' movement was feasible only because the organisation was not identified with any one political party, although clearly the activists were motivated by radical and left-wing ideals of social justice and equality. However, the movement gradually moved towards an alliance with the Labour Party and the Labour movement more generally. The postwar reforms made Labour seem the natural ally of the pensioners even though they remained in opposition for most of the 1950s. In 1964 the Labour Party won the General Election and a new era in the fortunes of the movement began. The election campaign signalled the Labour Party's commitment to improvements in state earnings-related pensions. There was increasingly clear identification of the pensioners' movement with the trade unions and the rights of working people.

One of the persistent divisions within the pensioners' movement has been between those who wish a close identification with the Labour and trade union movement and those who wish to keep their distance. In keeping its distance from parties, there were limits to the influence that the then NFOAPA (now Pensioners' Voice) could exert on the intra-party debates on policies and priorities. We can also see that the determination of the NFOAPA to remain aloof from political parties gave it the ability to distance itself from the Labour Party should it find its members' interests insufficiently taken into account. The NFOAPA survives by relying on its loyal members and not seeking financial and administrative support from wealthier and professionally organised groups. Although not the force it was, over the years, by relying on a dedicated core of loyal activists, and benefiting from the occasional windfall legacy, it has managed to publish a newspaper and stage a conference every year.

British Pensioners' Trade Union Action Association (BPTUAA)

The support of trade unionists has been crucial to the pensioners' movement since it began.[5] The current organisation most directly related to the trade unions is the British Pensioners' Trade Union Action Association (BPTUAA), founded in 1972. The desire of some pensioners for an active engagement with the Labour movement was formalised in the early 1970s, when a group of London dissidents formed the Camden Pensioners' and Trade Union Action Committee, joining forces thereafter with the London Joint Committee and the Scottish Pensioners' Association to form the BPTUAA. It has been suggested that this increasing interest in pensioners' issues was probably a response to both the first phase of the recession and Labour's loss of power in 1970. The main aims were to mobilise trade union support of pensioner causes and defend and improve state welfare generally. The BPTUAA is still in existence today and has 'over 32 national trade unions affiliated and estimates it has over 100,000 retired trade unionists and their partners in 400 branches, grouped into regions' (Ginn and Arber, 1999:161). The formation of the BPTUAA signalled both a renewed impetus in London and confirmed the shift in orientation of the pensioners' movement as a whole (Phillipson, 1982). Miles (1994:5-6) notes:

> The BPTUAA pursued a new strategy. They concentrated on pressing for policy change alongside sympathetic MPs and unions, aiming to set the agenda for a future Labour government via motions at the party conference.

Simultaneously at the start of the 1970s the Trade Union Congress (TUC) became interested in the pensions issue, a development for which Jack Jones, then the General Secretary of the Transport and General Workers Union (TGWU), is credited. Trade union support, and in particular the support of the leader of the TGWU, the UK's largest union,

---

[5] In 1902 George Barnes, General Secretary of the Amalgamated Society of Engineers, formed the National Committee of Organised Labour for Old Age Pension. Barnes spent the next three years travelling the country urging this social welfare reform. The measure was extremely popular and was an important factor in Barnes's being able to defeat Andrew Bonar Law, the Conservative cabinet minister in the 1906 General Election.

gave the pensioners' movement political weight with the Labour Party. As a result influence at the centre of government followed with the Labour electoral victories in 1974.

The National Pensioners' Convention (NPC)

The advantages to the pensioners' movement of having the support of the TUC were clear. Bornat (1998) says there were 'significant gains' for pensioner organisations through the 1970s. The National Pensioners' Convention (NPC) was formed in 1979 as an independent umbrella body, following a TUC initiative. It had a chequered history in the 1980s but was reconstituted in 1992 and is currently the central focus for campaigning pensioners. Supported by all of the main pensioners' organisations, it is constituted as an alliance of organisations, made up of affiliates such as Pensioners' Voice and the BPTUAA. In its reconstituted form it had support from the voluntary sector through Age Concern England, Help the Aged and the Centre for Policy on Ageing. It acknowledges the role of the TUC, Age Concern and Help the Aged in its foundation but is careful to declare itself an independent movement for pensioners.

The total affiliated membership has been estimated at about 1.5 million pensioners (Ginn and Arber, 1999:161). The NPC organises an annual Pensioners' Parliament, at which the concerns of the movement as a whole are voiced. It held its fifth Parliament in 2000. It has played an active role in consultations with government bodies, such as the Pensions Review, the Borrie Commission and the Royal Commission on Long Term Care. The aims of the NPC are clear: its main purpose has always been focused on a single issue, the demand for an adequate basic pension indexed to national average earnings. It has regional sections, as well as a national network of forums where older people can exchange views, and it helps set up new local forums for older people.

When it was first founded in 1979, the membership of the new organisation was almost entirely that of affiliated unions, notably the TGWU Retired Members' Association and the National Federation of Post Office and Telecom Pensioners. Later, Unison, Manufacturing Science Finance (MSF), GMB and the Civil Service Pensioners Alliance joined. It was an impressive alliance of forces. With sponsorship from, amongst others, Jack Jones, the NPC quickly established itself as a body with significant potential. The election of the Conservative government in 1979 was a blow to the unions, which not only lost an ally in government but were hit by legislation that threatened their financial base. With union funds under attack, the TUC, which had provided the major financial backing for the NPC, could no longer guarantee its support. Jack Jones, who subsequently became President of the NPC, recalls having to keep the organisation alive on a shoestring (OPPOL interview). The combination of economic change, which saw dramatic loss of employment in key mining and heavy industrial sectors where organised labour was most powerful, and a systematic campaign by the Conservative government to remove trade union power, led to a major loss of influence. These developments weakened the effectiveness of the new links made between the unions and the pensioners' organisations. This blow was one from which, despite the revival of the 1990s, the pensioners' movement has never fully recovered. Thus very soon after the establishment of the organisation, which had seemed to bring a powerful set of interests together in an alliance to campaign for pensioners, the NPC ceased to be a powerful and legitimate voice welcome in government policy-making forums.

The pensioners' movement began to gather an audience again as people experienced the erosion of the value of a core pillar of the welfare state, the basic pension, particularly from the late 1980s.[6] The BPTUAA's membership was considerably boosted in reaction to the Conservatives' policies and policy proposals, which threatened the value and predictability of retirement income for working people. In comparison to the NPC, the BPTUAA was and is a much more branch-oriented organisation rather than a national one. It therefore was able to recruit local activists opposed to the Thatcher government, but it didn't suffer the loss of representative function and prestige that the NPC, as an alliance of organisations, experienced with the change of government.

Campaigning on a Single Issue

Through the 1990s there has been an increase in pensioner activism, and the NPC has revived as an effective national coordinating body. The NPC as an umbrella organisation for a disparate group of people has based its solidarity on the single issue of restoring the link between the basic state pension and average male earnings. The campaigning success of the pensioners' movement had historically been dependent to a greater or lesser extent on its ability to elicit the sympathy of the wider population. Jack

---

[6] In the words of a London-based (OPPOL) interviewee, 'all hell was let loose as activists sought to challenge each step' of the 1986 Social Security Act. It was around this time also when effects of the changes to the state pension were being noticed. 'People were absolutely outraged in 1987 when the annual retirement pension increase was 40p. I mean the pensioners' movement, which began to gather an audience again. People really noticed the ludicrous sum of money being added to a core benefit for people. It also affected housing benefit, which brought it into sharp focus for many of those who, although poor, would not have seen pensions as an issue. A good assessment of the impact on different groups was published in the form of a leaflet entitled "Destroying Social Security" published by the Union Coalition for Social Security, for whom Tessa Jowell was the campaign organiser'.

Jones and the NPC successfully enlisted the support of respected 'concerned citizens' in the land for the '£75 in '99' campaign. A letter entitled 'Justice for Pensioners' calling for the basic pension to be raised to £75 was signed by Jack Jones, Michael Lake (Director General, Help the Aged) and Sally Greengross (Director General, Age Concern England) and published in the *Times* on 12 July 1999. Yet the campaign passed almost unnoticed by the general public. Nor was the 'restore the link' campaign making any discernible impact, despite the phrase having become the 'mantra' of the movement itself:

> The average man and woman in the street doesn't know much about it. You ask, '"Restore the link", what does it mean?' You say, "Restore the earnings link" – they think it means restoring the earnings of the individual ... if I say that to my colleagues, they think I am arguing against the campaign. I'm not. I would like to see the link restored, but I don't think it's the only thing. It wasn't the only thing in '74 – the big thing then was the 30% increase in the basic pension. (Jack Jones, President NPC, OPPOL interview)

Pensioners' campaigns are successful only if they strike a chord with the public – if, in effect, the wider population empathises with them. When this chord reverberates across party lines, as it did in 1994 with the campaign surrounding value added tax (VAT) on fuel, and in the editors' offices of the popular press, then success is much more likely. The 'restore the link' campaign has failed to catch fire in the same way in the face of repeated intransigence from senior politicians of both major parties and from the Treasury. Frustration on this key point of solidarity for the NPC has fuelled an increasingly bitter mood of soul-searching within the movement as to its future direction. The public empathised with the pensioners when the meagre 75p increase in the pension based on indexation to price inflation was announced. The government in response increased a variety of benefits – winter fuel payments, the Minimum Income Guarantee (MIG), television licence concessions. It pledged more money than it would have taken to restore the link to earnings – as the NPC had demanded – but it steadfastly refused to concede the principle.

The sense that growing numbers of pensioners ought to be politically effective, combined with frustration at their ability to influence government, has led to diverging opinions on the way forward. There was, for example, a widening rift between those who saw the unions as essential to the movement and those who felt that the organisational structure of the NPC privileged unions to the detriment of the movement. Central to this argument was the perception of the 'affiliated' unions as not providing sufficient funds to deserve their dominant position within the NPC Full

Council.[7] The NPC itself relied on Lottery money to run its London office in Chalfont Street, which brought it closer to charity status,[8] a position that might potentially compromise its ability to challenge government. Bruce Kent, who championed the idea of individual membership of the NPC, made clear when addressing activists in Manchester Town Hall (15 June 1999) and repeated in an interview:

> I think it's a democratic right. I think one ought to have a right in any national movement to have [an individual membership] and there is no problem about the process ... large groups that were federated to us have voting powers according to their numbers ... individual membership does not mean that you are on equal footing with the Transport and General Workers; you should have weighted input. (Bruce Kent, independent campaigner, OPPOL interview)

The argument for broadening the constituency of the movement, and raising funds by means of individual subscription fees, highlighted the need to change the Constitution of the NPC, which inhibited the movement's achieving just the sort of broad base needed:

> The constitution prescribes that organisations which affiliate to us are pensioner organisations. So that means that the level of affiliation is limited – we can't bring other organisations in. We can seek some support from other groupings and we certainly try to do that in terms of, say, churches; we've approached them to back our work. We can try to gain some level of spoken support in terms of letters and things like that, but we are a little bit stymied at the moment by not being able to include other organisations. (Gary Kitchen, NPC National Organiser, OPPOL interview)

These debates in the pensioners' movement about strategy, how to exert pressure and which alliances to seek and maintain are common to all pressure groups. What is significant about these debates at this time is that they reveal not a growing empowerment of older people but a sense of frustration at marginalisation. The increased activism and levels of campaigning in response to the erosion of the value of the state pension had

---

[7] The NPC Full Council is akin to the TUC, inasmuch as it is dominated by the major 'affiliated' unions; the TGWU Retired Members' Association, the National Federation of Post Office and Telecom Pensioners, Unison, MSF, GMB, and the Civil Service Pensioners' Alliance are the most influential. At the time of the OPPOL study, national organisations, no matter how large, paid affiliation fees of a maximum of £500 p.a., and regional organisations a maximum of £200 p.a.

[8] The links between lottery money and charities are very close, as is understood from the fact that Jill (Baroness) Pitkeathley, after ten years as chief executive of the Carers' National Association, joined the Opportunities Fund board responsible for distributing lottery money.

not met with tangible results and, despite a change in government, pensioners' organisations were not major players in policy formation.

Trade Union Links and Party Affiliation

Thus the pensioners' movement does not exclusively owe its existence to the trade unions. That said, its membership is predominantly made up of people with a trade union background. Indeed, without the support of the unions, and of the Retired Members' Associations in particular, there would be very little in the way of a national organised movement. Even those organisations that retain a 'no political affiliation' stance tend to reveal, in their *modus operandi* if nothing else, a debt to the trade unions. Pensioners' Voice, for example, has a formal written Constitution and branch structure that are unmistakably similar to those typical of trade unions.

The NPC has largely supplanted the NFOAPA as the dominant national organisation, and this has placed the trade unions at the heart of the movement as a whole. The NPC claims to represent older people generally, and to have over one million older people directly associated with the organisation. In this capacity it acts 'as an umbrella organisation when making representations to the government, Members of Parliament, Members of the European Parliament, Health Authorities and other statutory and voluntary bodies dealing with matters affecting pensioners' (NPC leaflet).

However, as an 'umbrella' organisation, the NPC has a system of deciding on resolutions that owes more to the traditional Labour movement's system of block votes than it does to grassroots democracy. The system of representation used by the NPC is distinctly that of the TUC, wherein the affiliated organisations have delegates on the Full National Council who debate and vote on motions raised at meetings throughout the year. Given the dominance of the unions in the NPC's affiliated membership system, it is clear that it is the sectional interests of the unions, more precisely the Retired Members' Associations of the unions, that largely define the nature of the decisions taken by the Executive. The one important vehicle for individual expression is the annual Pensioners' Parliament, which invites participation from all pensioners.

> It's open to anybody, any pensioner who wants to come along. It's a three-day event. It costs just a pound. It's a nominal charge, although people obviously have to pay their expenses to get to Blackpool. We have that annually and the last one was in May. As I said, we had two thousand pensioners attending, literally from throughout the UK – Scotland, Ireland, Wales and of course throughout England. (Gary Kitchen, National

Organiser, NPC, OPPOL interview)

Similarly, Pensioners' Voice has a strict Constitution that follows the trade union style. It is apparently very difficult to amend it, and it was clear from the sometimes rather tedious protocol of their annual conferences that any deviation from either the Constitution or the Standing Orders (overseen by a Standing Orders Committee) is frowned upon and gives rise to prolonged discussion. During the 1999 Annual Conference, the president herself seemed very aware of the need to allow more open discussion than was possible under the rules governing procedure, and this led to possibly the most stimulating and lively discussion of the conference, that concerning the government's Green Paper on Care for the Elderly.

It is possible to conclude that the long history of the organised pensioners' movement carries a legacy of organisational and constitutional complexity that inhibits its activities as a pressure group in the fast-moving, media-dominated contemporary political arena. This feature itself stems from the wide range of different interests within the older population as well as differences of ideology and tactics. The consequences are relatively effective local groups, where there are committed activists, but comparative difficulty in mounting nationally initiated and coordinated activity. These features may also be linked with problems of leadership and succession. Leadership of the pensioners' movement is not a career move for aspiring politicians or trade union leaders. It falls to professional leaders, such as trade union leaders, who have acquired a reputation for leadership in a previous career to take up the leadership of the pensioners' movement when they retire. Thus Rodney Bickerstaff of UNISON is to follow Jack Jones of the TGWU as President of the NPC. Retired leaders may have skills, strong reputations and connections, but they also have a natural time limit to their availability.

The Lifestyle-Oriented Associations

There are a large number of organisations in Britain that seek directly or indirectly to improve the lifestyle of older people. In doing this, they may be encouraging social activity and providing services, sometimes commercial services (such as holidays) and sometimes services targeted at specific social groups (for example, those over 50). Amongst the most visible of these is the Saga group of companies, which provides not only holidays but a widely read magazine. These 'lifestyle' organisations may be actively engaged in campaigning for such things as legislation prohibiting age discrimination in employment while refraining from taking an overtly political stance. This is in keeping with the stance of organisations such as the Carers' National Association (CNA), which calls itself a non-party political organisation while it 'hammers away at politicians for the furtherance of its policies' (*British Pensioner*, Winter 1998:9). In other words, it is apparent that a wide range of groups adopt an approach that combines proselytising with a determinedly apolitical stance. The Association of Retired People and those over 50 (ARP/O50) is probably the largest and most rapidly growing. Their stance on political involvement is clear from the following statement:

> It has always been the policy of ARP/O50 to collaborate with all political parties in forwarding the interests of older citizens and to avoid the temptation of believing that we possess political power in our own right. In a country with a 'first past the post' electoral system our chances of securing parliamentary representation are inevitably small even if we commanded uniform support among the eighteen million members of our own age group ... ARP/O50 believes that in order to gain greater political representation in the UK, seniors should actively engage the support and collaboration of the entire electorate across the political spectrum. (ARP/O50, website www.arp.org.uk, 12 July 1998)

ARP/O50 tends to accentuate the sophistication and independence of older people, whose rights it portrays as those of discerning consumers, and clearly targets a somewhat more affluent constituency than, for example, the NPC does. At the same time, it is an organisation that pays particular attention to the plight of what it calls 'the nearly poor':

> The retired population can be divided into roughly four groups. At the bottom are those who receive only the State pension and do not claim Income Support or the new Minimum Income Guarantee (MIG) ... this group numbers approximately 700,000. Those claiming MIG number 1.47 million, and, with additions such as Council Tax rebates and Housing Benefit, are a little better off. At the top are those who pay tax at 40% – all 150,000 of them. If these figures are deducted from the total current pensioner population of 10.5 million, we are left with roughly 8 million 'in the middle'. (Don Steele, Executive Director of ARP/O50, *Goodtimes*, October-November 1999:71)

Many charities and organisations show an increasing agility in being able to juggle the agenda of a voluntary sector organisation and that of a market-oriented business venture. Ultimately there is no real conflict, it seems, between mounting a campaign to challenge ageism with one hand and selling insurance with the other. Presenting older people as consumers of goods and services, capable of identifying their own needs and preferences, is a trend observable in public policy, academic publications and the agendas of a certain range of older people's organisations. This reflects a growing awareness of the potential of older people as informed and discerning consumers, an attitude that government has been keen to be seen to promote, for example through Better Government for Older People (BGOP), and the promotion of 'consumer' voices in local government services (see pages 60-2 for an extended discussion of BGOP).

The prediction that older people would become more active as a consumer group, more articulate in their demands and more determined to see them met, has long been a feature of the literature on older people (Neugarten, 1974; Phillipson, 1982). A report by Age Concern in the South West (1999:17) emphasised 'The Grey Market' and stated that 'people over 50 are the only growing sector of the UK population and account for 30% of consumer spending, they have 60% of total savings and possess almost an 80% share of the UK wealth. Together they have an annual income in excess of £166 billion.' Undoubtedly the perception of older people as a potential market is gaining ground, aided by reports in national papers such as that in the *Times* (27 July 1999) entitled 'Spend, spend, pensioners are the new rich'.[9]

The perception of a new generation of older people, with a sophisticated sense of its own value and power, is widespread – George Mudie, the government's Minister for Lifelong Learning, referred to 'the baby boom generation who, by their spending power, altered society, forced agencies and industries to take note of their wishes and needs' (Learning in Later Life Conference report, February 1999:3). Martin Shreeve, the Director of the BGOP programme, identified the '60s generation ... the consumer generation with fundamentally different expectations of quality of life' (OPPOL interview). The response of those organisations that are professionally interested in the welfare of older people, and share an interest in the financial situation of older people, is profoundly influenced by the idea that older people are going to form an increasingly demanding group.

The role of the business community and of 'sympathisers' in the press may prove to be crucial to the way in which issues affecting older people are presented in the future, and the wider public informed of their significance. These advocates do not necessarily campaign on behalf of older people, or encourage older people to take an active interest in issues relevant to them. However, the importance of their tacit support as opinion formers should not be underestimated. For example, the failure of the

---

[9] The simplistic tone of the headline belied a thoughtful article, based on research published by the Policy Studies Institute. The headline was later challenged in the article written by Don Steele, Executive Director of ARP/O50 and quoted above (*Goodtimes*, October-November 1999:71).

pensioners' movement to enlist the support of national newspaper editors can be seen as the single most important failing of the movement in its campaign to have the link between average earnings and the basic state pension restored – a campaign that has been running for over twenty years. Don Steele came to be Executive Director of the ARP/O50 from the ranks of the business community. Michael Lake, Director General of Help the Aged was previously a soldier, and Sally Greengross, now retired but formerly Director of Age Concern, came to the post after a career that started in business and academia. These are very different recruitment bases for leadership compared to those of the NPC. The next chapter reviews the impact of charities on the politics of old age.

4 Older People's Advocates – The Charities

Introduction

Older peoples' politics in Britain is wider than merely organisations of pensioners. There is a wider social movement that incorporates large numbers of voluntary organisations. Charitable organisations which have the well being of older people as their prime objective have come to be politically significant organisations playing a key role as advocates for older people.

The Charities

The two major UK charities for older people, namely, Age Concern and Help the Aged, dominate public understanding of older people and their interests. These two charities are frequently confused with each other and exhibit a considerable rivalry. Their origins are quite distinct, but over time their activities and organisational forms seem to have coincided more and more. This convergence has much to do with the changing perception of old age and older people, which means that the charities are keen to be seen to be encouraging active ageing, not promoting ageing stereotypes, and taking the role of facilitators rather than speaking for older people.

Age Concern has reinvented itself at least three times. It started at much the same time as the NFOAPA and was one of the successful group of lobbyists pressing the pensions issue during the Second World War (as discussed on pages 28-9). The Old People's Welfare Committee (OPWC) was led by Eleanor Rathbone and was formed with support from the National Council for Social Service in response to a request from the new National Assistance Board. In 1944 the OPWC adopted the title National Old People's Welfare Committee (NOPWC) to distinguish it from the growing number of local committees. It tried throughout the 1950s to coordinate the voluntary-sector provision for older people, which local government increasingly funded, and during the 1960s expanded its service development and policy advisory roles. The reform of social services and local government in the early 1970s significantly changed the role of voluntary organisations in the provision of 'old people's welfare'. The name Age Concern England was adopted, and many local committees also took the name. Recently the organisation engaged in further constitutional reform to try to accommodate its charitable, advocacy, policy research and advice roles, and its accountability to older people. It changed its Constitutional title to the National Council on Ageing, and now brings together eighty-five national organisations concerned with ageing as well as representatives of over a thousand local Age Concern organisations. Its 1998/9 income was almost £30 million but this figure does not include the activities of local Age Concern groups, which are formally independent of the national organisation. It remains the single most powerful voice of older people addressing government.

Help the Aged is a very large charity, with an income of a little over £40 million in 1998/9. It was founded in 1961 with a remit to respond to the needs of poor, frail and isolated older people at home and overseas. Its international activities, carried on by a separate arm of the organisation, have been a distinctive feature of its work. As a national organisation they describe themselves as campaigning with and on behalf of older people, raising money to help pensioners in need and providing direct services where they have identified a gap in provision. They also aspire to provide a coordinating role for the many local charitable institutions directed at older people. In addition they have established and seek to maintain local groups of supporters and forums to articulate the concerns of older people.

The history of the pensioners' movement discussed in the previous chapter is the history of a movement that has tried to challenge government policy without having to rely on intermediaries. Independence from political parties in particular has been the stated aim of most organisations within the movement. Independence from the voluntary charitable sector is, however, no less problematic a goal than that of achieving independence from political parties or trade unions. The increasing dominance of the charitable sector in the role of older people's advocate has not met with unanimous approval, as it suggests that older people themselves have become increasingly dependent on unaccountable organisations in lobbying government. In the 1980s, for example, academic Chris Phillipson advocated that older people should be more reliant 'on their own organisations to challenge economic and social policies' (1982:102).

The objectives of the pensioners' movement and those of the charities overlap to a considerable extent. The charities go to considerable lengths to consult older people on their priorities. Age Concern conducted various consultation exercises to determine its own mission and aims. For example in Wales, Age Concern Cymru has effectively collated the results of various initiatives they have facilitated (the 'Listening Event' in Cardiff) or directly organised (the Millennium Debate of the Age)[10] designed to discover older people's priorities. While the charities are acutely conscious of the need to avoid patronising older people, the fact remains that the major charities are enormously wealthy in comparison to organisations of older people. No matter how successful they are in facilitating the representation of older people's interests, they are perceived by government and the general public as ambassadors for a population that is only influential when supported by professional organisations.

Bridging the Gap Between Pensioners and the Government

Traditionally the organisations that represent pensioners fall into two distinct categories: those in which older people themselves are the members and that are run by elected officers and those that are staffed by professionals who are responsible to a Board of Trustees. The two forms of representation are significantly different. The latter, with a top-down structure, is suited to the fast pace of Parliamentary decision making and party policy formation; the former is restricted by a Constitution to a form of representative decision making that can be both tedious and time consuming.

The determinedly democratic and grassroots representation of pensioners by pensioners exhibited by the pensioners' movement contrasts vividly with the representation of pensioners by those organisations that campaign on behalf of them (Walker, 1992b). However, the charities have proved themselves capable of bridging the gap between Parliament and the wider public of older people, and effective at both operating within the corridors of Westminster and keeping in touch with grassroots opinion.[11] At the same time, the charities are, by definition, unable to adopt just the sort of overtly political and campaigning stance that has characterised the pensioners' movement. Age Concern obtained a special dispensation from the Charity Commissioners to provide a research assistant to the Parliamentary All-Party Group on Ageing and Older People. That said, the major charities have acquired considerable influence within the political system, and effectively provide the most efficient means of publicising the concerns of older people and providing information to Parliament and the

---

[10] The Director of Age Concern Cymru described the activities associated with the debate as achieving 'a lot of common outcomes' and commented that the 'People's Voices' initiative, devised by the Wales Debate Committee, suggested that 'ordinary people's view, the layperson's view, young or old, appears to be about the same on what the issues are' (OPPOL).

[11] This is 'the gap between the great inside and the great outside' identified by Antony Sampson (1971).

media. Inevitably they are consulted by government and the media on issues relevant to the welfare of older people, and make pronouncements on government policy.

Collaborating in government consultation exercises means that the charities both legitimise government initiatives and facilitate better government understanding of older people's needs. All in all, it appears that, by entering into 'partnership' arrangements with government, industry and commerce, 'charities are an expanding political force' (Stansfield, 1999:3). Age Concern has six press officers readily on hand to liase with Parliament or the media, two campaign workers, two policy officers and two Parliamentary officers. Age Concern has the ability, therefore, by means of its Parliamentary officers in particular, to brief politicians on the results of surveys and research that it regularly commissions. They can arrange for ministers to attend meetings the aim of which is to discuss government policy for a wider audience of interested professionals, mainly drawn from the voluntary sector.

Its policy officers are responsible for servicing the All Party Group in Parliament,[12] which deals with issues relevant to older people, providing 'a forum within the House of Commons for discussion and campaigning on issues affecting pensioners' (House of Lords, 1991). This forum is a key route by which the charities are able to lobby for changes to policy. For example, in 1994 the All Party Group lent its weight to the campaign to withdraw the VAT increase on fuel.[13]

Campaigning within Charitable Status

Modern charities are designed to raise money and perform practical services that are beneficial for a section of the community, not to exert power to achieve political objectives. They cannot wheel and deal as power brokers or flex political muscle to achieve their ends. In accordance with general legal principles, however, charities may still engage in political

---

[12] In 1970 a group of MPs was formed in the House of Commons to deal with pensioner problems, and a similar group formed in the House of Lords. In 1998 the House of Commons All Party Group for Older People and the House of Lords All Party Group on Ageing merged to form the All Party Parliamentary Group on Ageing and Older People. With over one hundred members drawn from all three major parties, the Group has consistently tabled questions on the 'incomes of different groups of pensioners, and called repeatedly for the pension to be increased' (Annual Report, 1992). As a cross-party group its influence on the government of the day may be diluted, but its 1992 Annual Report stated that 'there is considerable cross-party agreement on the need for substantial increases, and this remains a priority of the Group's work'.

[13] The most dramatic government *volte-face* in recent years – the decision implemented in April 1994 raising VAT from 8% to 17.5% – was rescinded in November the same year.

activities provided that these are purely ancillary to the main objectives of the charity. The exact limits to what a charity can and cannot do on behalf of a given population are, therefore, far from clear. Consequentially they are able to support the demands made by pensioners and can take a lead in presenting arguments to government, but they will refrain from becoming identified with the pensioners' movement *per se*.

The charities gain widespread support for their campaigns to end age discrimination within the National Health Service (NHS), as for example with Age Concern's campaign 'Dignity on the Ward'. They do not, however, attack with the same conviction the underlying social inequalities that determine the sort of healthcare elderly patients receive. Their priority tends to be directed to those who are in immediate need, or are particularly vulnerable, rather than the generality of older people. This is understandable, given the fact that the Charity Commission's guidelines do not permit charities to engage in activities designed to bring pressure on the government to adopt a particular course of action. Ultimately the charities tend to 'depoliticise' the situation of older people. Phillipson (1982) notes the damping down of the fires that the pensioners' movement has fought to keep alight, and similarly campaigner Bruce Kent suggests that 'in this country charitable status is actually a means of quietening activists' (OPPOL interview).

The charities do not seek to influence the result of elections but do seek to influence policy. Age Concern releases its own manifesto before each election; it is 'publicly available and circulated to all candidates of major parties standing in the election' (Sally Greengross, Director General Age Concern, OPPOL interview). Local Age Concern groups may also run hustings for candidates in their local constituency. Crucially, what they cannot do is recommend to people how to vote, or devise electoral strategies to seek to achieve a majority for a particular political party. However, information is power. The charities engage in and sponsor research and disseminate the findings. A good example is the way the government's policy was questioned by the report of the Study Group on Paying for Age. This panel of experts was assembled to inform the debate on the affordability of the pensions system within the broad scope of other issues addressed in the Millennium Debate of the Age (which Age Concern initiated). Another means the charities find by which to express dissatisfaction with government policy, and to lobby for change, is that of publicising the shortcomings of provision made for older people in the pages of their Parliamentary bulletins.[14] For example, both Help the Aged

---

[14] Age Concern's *Reportage*, Help the Aged's *Policy Update*, and the Abbeyfield Society's *Parliamentary News* are three examples.

and Age Concern have consistently used their bulletins to criticise the government for dragging its feet in responding to the Royal Commission's recommendations on long-term care for the elderly. This information can be extremely important in picking out key issues for older people through detailed analysis of documents and keeping track of situations where decisions are delayed, or found to be contradictory or obscure.

The charities play an important role in collecting and disseminating information with which pensioners can support their demands on government. Where their roles as information gatherers and campaigners overlap most clearly is in the way they conduct surveys among older people and report their findings.[15] Research conducted by the charities substantiates and fuels the campaign for an increase in the basic state pension. The charities, whose credibility is assured and whose opinions carry weight with the media as well as with policy makers, are by such means able to lobby government, albeit indirectly. One example of a campaign designed to change government policy mounted by a charity was Age Concern's encouragement of the public to lobby their MPs to persuade them to sign an Early Day Motion (EDM) aimed at establishing an enquiry into the extent of age discrimination in the NHS (see *Network*, 7 July 1999:7).

Clearly, however, the charitable status of such organisations severely limits their activities in the political sphere.[16] It is possible that the charities feel more comfortable campaigning on issues such as the implementation of proposals outlined by the Royal Commission on Long Term Care[17] than on issues that address pensioner poverty through the redistributive role of the state. Whereas the NPC and other organisations concentrate on the pensions issue, charities adopt a broad-brush approach

---

[15] Conferences also provide the opportunity for the pensioners' movement to join forces with the major charities. For example, the 21st Century Care conference hosted by Help the Aged and the Greater London Forum for the Elderly in 1998 demonstrated how expert testimony lends weight to the arguments put by pensioners.

[16] Just how far they are constrained by the law on charitable status has a long and complex legal history. Some would say that the Commission's guidelines do actually allow considerable leeway (Reports, 1969, 1979, 1981, 1986, App. A (b)). However, the basic position stems from Bowman v. Secular Society Ltd. [1917] AC 406, when Lord Parker of Waddington summed up the basic position as follows:

A trust for the attainment of political objects has always been held invalid, not because it is illegal, for everyone is at liberty to advocate or promote by any lawful means a change in the law, but because the court has no means of judging whether a proposed change in the law will or will not be for the public benefit, and therefore cannot say that a gift to secure the change is a charitable gift.

[17] Established in December 1997, its report, drawing on extensive consultation, was published in March 1999.

to 'age-related' issues. In terms of the resources at their disposal, the charities are enormously more rich and powerful than are the pensioners' organisations. However, their different historical development, objectives and legal status give them as organisations related but different priorities. The determination of the charities to address a wide range of issues contrasts with the 'single issue' approach of the pensioners' movement. The charities feel particularly responsible for welfare provision and professional standards in health and social care. The pensioners' organisations are not unconcerned about these issues but, seeing themselves as representative organisations for senior citizens, they give priority to campaigning for their social rights as citizens – primarily the state pension. Where collaboration on the issue of pensions is seen between the charities and the pensioners' movement, the campaigns have not been noticeably more successful. For example, the '£75 in '99' campaign might have achieved some publicity but did not achieve its immediate goals. Faced with political intransigence from government, the charities cannot go beyond persuasion and into the realms of political mobilisation and arm twisting.

Alienating Pensioners and Encouraging Dependency Stereotypes

In promoting older people's needs, the charities also reinforce, albeit inadvertently, the image of older people as 'needy' – a cause for concern. There is a tension between, on the one hand, the fund-raising activities of the charities, utilising the compassion of the public for the vulnerable to raise money and promote their direct services for older people, and, on the other, anti-ageism campaigns with the need to counter stereotypes of older people as vulnerable and dependent. The charities are increasingly involved in marketing services (insurance, flowers, etc.) as fund-raising ventures. Thus, of necessity, commercial considerations become part of the calculation of their public activities and the controversy they provoke. It is, therefore, a fine line that the charities tread between bringing to public attention the sorts of indignities and general discrimination older people suffer, and portraying them as a dependent population. It is a dilemma of which the charities are themselves aware.

Poorer pensioners have come to rely on intermediaries in the voluntary sector, whose efforts during the 1940s the pensioners' movement had so consummately derided (Blaikie, 1990:33). Given the lack of resources that is a permanent feature of the pensioners' movement, there is obviously a good argument for having professionally run bodies such as Age Concern intercede on behalf of pensioners. The problem is that this sophisticated form of advocacy and lobbying is far removed from the sort of grassroots democracy and campaigning that the pensioners enjoy, and of which they are understandably proud. While it is clear that the major charities have the resources that allow them to lobby government in a professional manner, it is precisely their high level of professionalism, and the fact that they receive government funding, that alienates them from the pensioners who are members of organisations belonging to the pensioners' movement. The distinction between different forms of representation is important, therefore, not only because it draws attention to a lack of professional skills that hinders effective lobbying on the part of pensioners' organisations, but also because it reveals a potentially compromised legitimacy. Charitable status sets limits on what charities can do in the name of pensioners. For example, confrontational and conflictual strategies such as direct action are not options for organisations that depend on finance from government, business and private donations. As we write this in the autumn of 2000 it is clear that such direct action has proved effective for farmers and road hauliers in their campaign on the price of fuel.

Images of Older People Legitimised by Charities

There are many charitable organisations that act on behalf of and claim to represent older people. The problem of organisations *for* older people rather than *of* older people merely highlights older people's dependency on other people. These organisations implicitly define older adults as a category, like children, who *can't speak for themselves.* The whole concept of charitable organisations *for* older people differentiates older people from those who have full adult status.

The names of these organisations also manifest these concepts. The name Age Concern implies that older adults are a subject of concern, or anxiety. The name Help the Aged implies that older people *can't help themselves* and need our help. These groups are traditionally aligned with welfare, as there is no such thing as a charity that helps the self-sufficient. Organisations such as these contribute implicitly to the dependency stereotypes of older people. Unlike most discriminatory attitudes that adversely affect minority groups, benevolent but ageist attitudes have actually prompted public support for the elderly and improved their economic status. Organisations such as Age Concern and Help the Aged are very powerful. They make sure older people's issues are on the political agenda through direct consultation with the government and media campaigns that highlight the need for a sympathetic approach to creating social policy for the elderly. The political danger of the image of the dependent elderly is that they may come to be seen as an economic burden. It may also inhibit their own ability to act as an interest group with specific needs and voting power.

Other Groups

The organisational fragmentation of the social movement for older people is extended to the whole of the voluntary and charitable sector. Just as the distinctions and rivalries between pensioners' organisations are unclear in the mind of the public, so the rivalries and distinctions between the two major charities are also a source of confusion. Just as there is a multiplicity of pensioners' organisations, so there is also a wide range of other local and national charities concerned with local or specific old-age issues. The Anchor Trust, which has a primary interest in housing, conducts research and has participated in the Better Government for Older People (BGOP) initiative. Similarly, the Carnegie Third Age Programme has published an influential report and been engaged with BGOP. The Pre-Retirement Association is a charity particularly concerned with the transition from work to retirement and provides courses and conducts research directed at easing this process. The Employers Forum on Age 'promotes the business benefits of a mixed-aged workforce', seeking to combat age discrimination at work from within. It publishes, in conjunction with Age Concern, a newsletter for employers. This list is not intended to be definitive, but rather to illustrate the fragmentation and diversity of the voluntary sector.

Academics and their organisations have also often supported the pensioners' movement. Individual academics have taken significant roles in pensioners' organisations as well as provided information and written pamphlets. Professional associations such as, for example, the British Society for Gerontology, the British Geriatrics Society and the Royal College of Nursing, while existing primarily for their professional members, do also seek to advance the interests of their subjects, clients or patients by providing information and responding to consultation exercises. Research findings published by prestigious organisations such as the Centre for Policy on Ageing or the Age Concern Institute on Ageing carry weight with government and may be publicised in the media. Thus, in practice, the contemporary, broad-based pensioners' movement is a wide coalition of groups not dissimilar to the range of pensioners' organisations, voluntary organisations and academics who were influential in the origins of the state pension.

In recent years the rise in pensioner activism has been reflected in the development of a range of mechanisms to facilitate communication between pensioners and local and national government. These attempts to provide a mechanism by which the voices of unorganised pensioners can be heard are the topic of the following chapter.

5 Listening to Older People – Forums and Debates

Introduction

This chapter will look at the range and effectiveness of initiatives designed to strengthen lines of communication between senior citizens and government. It will look at diverse political mechanisms, some of which are recent innovations, and develop an overall perspective about the utility and political functions of these institutions.

Seniors' Forums

Seniors' forums started when activists in the pensioners' movement, 'responding to a continuous pattern of cuts and closures in health and social services' in the 1980s began forming themselves into protest groups in order to organise protests and mount local campaigns (Miles, 1994:6). Many of these local groups, particularly when they had local government sponsorship, took the title 'Forums', as in 'Forums for the Elderly' or 'Senior Citizens' Forums'.[18] Supported and encouraged by the voluntary sector and local government, forums have become increasingly influential, notably in London, Glasgow and some other major UK cities. Many informed commentators see them as a significant development; Tessa Harding, Head of Planning and Development with Help the Aged described them in the following terms:

> They have become increasingly influential, in London particularly. There are lots of local forums which play an important campaigning role. They use the material that we and others provide and that the National Pensioners' Convention itself centrally provides and they get very involved in local issues. They might be campaigning at any one time over the closure of residential homes or transport arrangements in the area and the availability of safe or reliable transport or concessionary fares or

---

[18] The names vary somewhat arbitrarily, although some variations express differences in relationship to sponsoring local authorities. Strathclyde has its 'Elderly Forum', Coventry its 'Older People's Forum', Devon an 'Advisory Group of Older People', while the NPC runs a network for 'Senior Citizens' Forums'.

whatever. (OPPOL interview)

Forums provide a vital opportunity for older people to organise into local lobby groups, and the spread of forums indicates grassroots activity is on the increase. Forums address a wide variety of issues and focus on local problems. Their priorities are inevitably determined to some extent by the local environment, sponsoring organisations, their history of activism and the realities of local provision. Pensioner activists we interviewed in Hackney may well be more overtly political in outlook than those from the London Borough of Sutton. Hackney has pensioner-led groups as well as a BGOP initiative called the 'Council for Older People'. Both places exhibited a level of local activism and commitment that has led Walker (1998) to suggest that these local groups might represent a significant new form of old-age politics. Their impact on national rather than local politics is less obvious. Nonetheless, forums do tend to offer an opportunity for local people to address national issues, and broad-based forum committees allow an extraordinary cross-pollination of agendas.

> My own local forum where I live in southeast London – our Chair is from Age Concern, and incidentally an active Liberal, and the two Vice-chairs, one is from the Transport and General Workers Retired Members' Association, the other is from a local black church, the Treasurer is from the British Legion, the delegate to the Greater London Forum is from the British Pensioners ... Now you see that's quite a mixture and it's amazing how well we all get on. (London pensioner activist, OPPOL interview)

The forums seem capable of involving a wide range of people who have a multitude of interests, concerns and needs. The enormous diversity of different kinds of forum and the proliferation of consultation initiatives with older people are phenomena that require explanation. One possible hypothesis is that they fill a communication gap between the political and administrative elites on the one hand, and older people on the other, which is felt by both sides.

Although the scale and resources of these charitable organisations tends to overshadow pensioners' organisations working within small budgets, they recognise the need for pensioners to have their own voice. The major charities are committed to acting as facilitators and do so by providing support to senior citizens' forums. Both Help the Aged and Age Concern have recently focused on engaging older people politically, training older people in campaign skills, involving older people in consultation processes and, in the case of Help the Aged, providing funds for older people to develop their own forums. Help the Aged, for example, allocated £250,000 of its UK Grants Programme to the establishment of forums in 1999.

Successful lobbying by older people depends on the support they receive from organisations that can offer resources unavailable to local pensioners' groups. Sponsorship by powerful organisations such as Help the Aged is a means of obtaining both funding and expertise. For example, critical to the success of older people as a lobby group is their ability to gain access to the media. Recognising that gaining this access has been a perennial problem for pensioners groups, Age Concern organised a series of workshops designed to improve the situation of those in the pensioners' movement who were interested in this aspect of campaigning. The Greater London Forum, for example, took advantage of the scheme in 1999.

The Greater London Forum for the Elderly (GLF)

One of the most well-established and influential forums is the Greater London Forum for the Elderly. The GLF is the umbrella organisation for forums covering the entire metropolitan region of London. It was established while the Greater London Council (GLC), led by Ken Livingstone,[19] was a focus of opposition to Margaret Thatcher's Conservative government. The idea survived the Conservatives' abolition of the GLC, the successor forum being established in 1988 by Harry Kay. Tony Carter, a former Chair of the GLF, described the way the forums emerged in the 1980s:

> Forums started about twelve years ago now, and they started in London and, coincidentally – as far as I have discovered, there wasn't any connection – about the same time in the Strathclyde region of Scotland. The reason they started in London was because the GLC, whose leader is someone you might have heard of, Ken Livingstone. He was then the leader of the GLC and he was a friend to us because he was very much influenced by another man, sadly now dead, Harry Kay, who was a great pensioners' leader and who in turn was a friend of Jack Jones. Jack had already worked out the idea of a forum, and he and Harry persuaded the GLC that they were not hearing the voice of older people, and so the old GLC and the then pensioners' organisations in London set up consultative machinery ... Soon after that, sadly, the GLC was abolished by Mrs Thatcher, but the consultative machinery, or at least the pensioners' side of it, remained and it became the Greater London Forum for the Elderly. (OPPOL interview)

---

[19] 'The big boost in the mid-eighties for the activists in London was certainly the support of Ken Livingstone and the GLC...and so for two or three years the GLC actually sponsored the pensioners' movement demos...and that gave the activists quite a shot in the arm...' (interview with an informed London-based advocate for older people).

By the early 1990s the forums in London had gained a firm foothold in local government in boroughs such as Lewisham:

> What happened between the summer of 1990 and April 1992 is that actually the new realists, particularly the forums movement, gained ground ... One of the difficulties for the pensioners' movement is that it has often done well only with what you could call a sponsoring partner. So if Lewisham Council decided to offer the pretty privileged consultative framework that it offered Lewisham pensioners' forum, then people are going to get seriously involved. Here was something where you could get local bus routes rerouted, you could defend the standard of services to day centres and so on. (London community worker, OPPOL interview)

One definition of a forum and its purpose is: 'A borough Forum is an umbrella body composed of representatives of older people's organisations and other bodies working with or for older people in that borough. A Forum's main concern is representing their own views to their local authority, MPs, MEPs and other statutory/voluntary bodies' (GLF leaflet, May 1999). The GLF seeks to make older people visible politically. In encouraging people to see themselves as part of something that can offer such an opportunity, the GLF is playing a very significant role in helping to generate a momentum towards a specific representational route for older people. There are now Senior Citizens' Forums in all thirty-three London boroughs.

The forums are, therefore, specifically aimed at providing a voice for older people, and a vehicle by which to express their views and organise campaigns. One such campaign was the 'Right to Vote!', in which the GLF in 1998 joined forces with a wide range of voluntary-sector groups to call on political parties and candidates to guarantee that public meetings be held in accessible locations, to make campaign literature available in different formats and generally to seek 'new ways to ensure that all citizens have the opportunity to participate actively in the democratic process' (GLF Annual Report, 1999:8).

Forums also contribute to empowering the minority communities. Since 1997, when the Executive Committee established the Black and Ethnic Minority (BEM) Elders' Working Group, it has been the policy of the GLF to raise the profile of ethnic minorities within the organisation. In September 1999 the BEM Elders' Working Group collaborated with other London-wide pensioner organisations to set up the Minority Ethnic Black Elders' Strategic Alliance (MEBESA). One of the main concerns of the BEM Working Group is to foster a good relationship with service providers. Conferences, such as the National Service Framework for Older

People (May 1999) and the conference hosted with the GLF on the Crime and Disorder Act (June 1999) are opportunities for this to happen.

Networking and collaborating with a wide range of organisations is an essential part of the role of forums. The GLF is part of many London-wide groups and alliances, including the London Health Alliance, the Transport Committee for London, the Travel Permit Working party, the London Mobility Advisory Panel and the London Carers' Network. It has links with the Social Policy Action Network convened by Help the Aged, and it worked with church groups and others to help coordinate facilities and a database for Millennium Year activities. The GLF also formed part of the Advisory Committee for the Speaking Out project run by Age Concern.

Forums are able to follow developments in government policy from an informed vantage point. Sponsorship from charities and local government provides knowledge, expertise and good downward communication. In turn, these organisations obtain credibility through their contact with pensioners' organisations. This reciprocal arrangement means that the issues that inform the agendas of the voluntary sector also inform those of the forums, thereby maintaining synergies that are conducive to powerful (because they are based on the real needs of the older population) representations to government. An illustration of the positive nature of this relationship is found in the Report of the '21st Century Care – Older People Have Their Say' conference held in June 1999, jointly organised by the GLF and Help the Aged. This document details the real needs of older people in this area and conveys the urgency of the situation.

From their own annual review of their work it is possible to gain an appreciation of how busy these forums are in fulfilling their aims, and how, as part of a network, they represent an increasingly vocal and active presence within the pensioners' movement as a whole. For example, the Brent Pensioners' Forum in 1998 reported attending the National Pensioners' Day March and Rally to Trafalgar Square, a Poster Parade along Oxford Street organised by the Greater London Pensioners' Association, and a rally held at Central Hall Westminster at which high-profile speakers, including Barbara Castle, Tony Benn and Jack Jones, addressed an audience of over a thousand pensioners, with another thousand lending their support outside. Clearly the membership of these forums is politicised, despite the fact that the 'Forums are non-party political' (*Greater London Pensioner*, May 1999). They will actively campaign as forums on an overtly political brief; for example, the Harrow Pensioners' Action Association campaigned for better pensions 'by supporting the lobbies of the House of Commons organised by the GLPA, writing to our MPs and informing the local press of our activities' (*Greater London Pensioner*, May 1999:17).

Pensioners do seem to be better at local community activity than they are at nationally coordinated campaigns. The '21st Century Care – Older People Have Their Say' report suggested that 'older people are actively involved in community activities and are willing to stand up for their rights, but they won't necessarily push nationally without encouragement'.

Forums can enable their members, as part of networks headed by umbrella bodies that have professional staff, to join their voices and participate in national policy formation exercises. Nationwide coordination is a major problem for active pensioner groups. In large urban areas at least, there seems the possibility of genuine grassroots activism using forums and their resources for a more effective voice. The extent to which forums can be more than debating chambers and take action and exercise power over decisions made by local and national government must remain an open question. They can clearly be a tool for more effective local government; whether they can have any impact on national decision making is far more problematic.

Facilitating Public Debate

Millennium Debate of the Age

In 1996, Age Concern England established the Debate of the Age. The Debate conducted 'the largest programme of deliberative public consultation ever carried out anywhere in the world' (Opinion Leader Research, 1999). The programme was launched in March 1998, ran for eighteen months, and included two nation-wide surveys, focus groups, twelve Citizens' Juries and the UK's first Citizens' Forum. The Debate employed two key 'deliberative' elements, the Citizens' Juries and the Citizens' Forum, the former providing the 'real meat of the consultation process'. Twelve Juries involving between twelve and eighteen people, and sometimes different age groups, were consulted in twelve regions, the subjects under consideration having been determined in advance by focus groups. This so-called 'bottom-up' approach, allied with questionnaires and reports, was intended to involve non-expert testimony and opinion. The Citizens' Juries and the larger Citizens' Forum were asked to consider specific questions such as pensions policy. The largest single event was the Citizens' Forum held in Birmingham in June 1999. In this way the Debate demonstrated, according to Opinion Leader Research (1999), the ability of older people to make a valuable contribution to policy making as 'ordinary citizens'.

The results of these consultative exercises formed the basis of propositions that were further discussed at a series of conferences in the autumn of 1999, culminating in a set of Millennium Papers, which were produced by the Debate of the Age study groups. The Debate itself was wound up in London in December 1999, with around a thousand participants asked to set priorities from a list of thirty-five proposals. Meanwhile Help the Aged had been conducting its own consultative exercise, entitled 'Speaking Up for Our Age', culminating in a conference held in Westminster on 23 June 1999.

> This national event has followed seven regional conferences as part of a Help the Aged programme to encourage older people to make their voices heard ... Delegates at the conferences were encouraged to set up local groups and discussed how to get their voices heard in the media. (*Policy Update*, 12 August 1999)

Although the Debate of the Age proclaimed 'cross-party support' and had been endorsed by each of the party leaders, the results appear to have had little direct impact. The Debate's findings were laid out in the Millennium Papers, many of which clearly challenged the government to adjust its policies. It is asserted in the 'Paying for Age in the 21st Century' paper produced for the Debate that 'the most important source of pressure on governments is an informed electorate'. It remains to be seen whether such debates do in practice enhance the ability of older people to influence government. There are two ways of looking at these consultative exercises. First, there is the view that they play a very important part in the setting of agendas (for example, Age Concern Wales's elaboration of the Pensioners' Manifesto). The other view is that they are really no more than elaborate public relations exercises, which reiterate the importance of the major charities as facilitators and the government's willingness to hear opinions, but do not change the balance of power that produces older people's current conditions.

As discussed above, in recent years governments and parties have made sure that through their consultation procedures they are seen to provide a means by which older people can have a voice. Many government and local authority bodies have introduced forums whereby older people can be consulted – the Better Government for Older People initiatives are an example. A number of charities and other organisations have developed advocacy schemes for frail elderly people. However, in some sense such moves are indicative of marginalisation and lack of power. They indicate, rather than a growing electoral power of older voters, a felt need to take action to make sure that they are not further marginalised.

The Response of Parliamentarians: All Party Groups and Committees

The way the organised pensioners' movement makes itself felt at
Westminster reflects the pattern of politics in the House of Commons.
There are debates in the Commons and the Lords, specialist committees
and lobbying activities. Chamber debates are generally set pieces, and party
political considerations dominate. Government Ministers are loath to be
seen to accept ideas and representation from those on the Opposition
benches who raise older people's issues. Beyond the Commons and the
Lords, there are a whole range of procedures and groups that allow interests
and pressure groups to be felt within the Palace of Westminster. Standing
Committees, which deal with legislation as it passes through Parliament,
look at bills line by line, clause by clause. These committees, made up from
all the parties, examine the bill, and amendments by members on both sides
are brought forward. Such committees combine both the public and the
private backbench role. The public activity consists of speeches to the
Committee, which are recorded in Hansard just as the debates in the
Chamber are.[20] The private side occurs at the beginning of the week when
the committee is meeting; a private meeting with the ministerial team is
held at which 'as a backbencher you will be able to raise a number of
issues' (Charlotte Atkins, MP). There are also Select Committees, which
are permanent Committees with Chairs who are independent of
government, and which can and do vigorously scrutinise the activity of
government and investigate controversial issues.

The pensioners' movement has its champions in the House of
Commons, but they are for the most part backbench MPs whose influence
on government policy is limited. Yet it is these individuals who, in
supporting the pensioners' attempts to organise as a pressure group,
provide the pensioners' movement with some limited sense of efficacy.
Some of the MPs who support the movement show the same tenacity for
which the movement's leaders are renowned. Paul Flynn, for example, has
used the Early Day Motion (EDM), considered a very insignificant tool by
most,[21] to good effect:

> Now Paul Flynn, who is a splendid ally of ours and a wonderful MP of
> whom I can't speak too highly, has for the last couple of years made sure

---

[20] Hansard is the official record of Parliament and publishes verbatim transcripts of
debates.

[21] According to the *Daily Telegraph* the EDM is a 'piffling thing', which should be
viewed as an irrelevance to the real business of government. According to the paper, Charles
Kennedy, leader of the Liberal Democrats, made a fool of himself by asking the Prime
Minister if he had read the EDM on pensions which eighty-five Labour MPs had signed (12
February 2000:12).

that at the beginning of the Parliamentary session, which means immediately after the Queen's speech, that he goes along to the House of Commons at some incredibly early hour the following morning and is the first in the queue to get his EDM down before anybody else. That is then EDM number one and it remains EDM number one for the whole of that Parliamentary session ... and this means that every time a member signs it, it not only appears on the order paper, it appears at the top of the order paper, and so Paul Flynn's EDM calling for the basic pension to be increased to £75 has appeared at the top of the order paper on a large number of occasions in the past year. (Tony Lynes, Pensions Expert, NPC, OPPOL)

The use of the EDM does, whatever its failings, provide a means of signalling disaffection from within the ranks of Labour backbenchers. Another method of gaining the attention of government ministers is the Adjournment Debate:

You can get your own private adjournment debate, which lasts half an hour, and you get as a backbencher fifteen minutes to speak, which is a long time actually, but more importantly you get a fifteen-minute response from the Minister. (Charlotte Atkins, MP, OPPOL)

With its historic links, the pensioners' movement has natural allies among the Parliamentary Labour Party and the large trade union group within Parliament. Through interested MPs, the pensioners' movement has, in theory, a channel to government ministers. However, such channels do not necessarily mean that older peoples' voices achieve significant impact. For example, the Select Committee system is a key parliamentary mechanism for holding the executive to account. The problem for the pensioners' movement is that those MPs who are most capable of representing its interests are not necessarily placed by the Labour party's Whips on these committees where they would be most influential. Party managers do not see it as part of their function to facilitate critical voices. Only the All Party Groups provide, ultimately, an ongoing forum for a serious airing of the pensioners' movement perspective in Parliament.

In 1998 the House of Commons All Party Group for Older People and the House of Lords All Party Group on Ageing merged to form the All Party Parliamentary Group on Ageing and Older People, which aimed to provide 'a forum within the House of Commons for discussion and campaigning on issues affecting pensioners' (Annual Report, 1991). As a cross-party group its influence on the government of the day may be diluted, but its 1992 Annual Report, referring to pensions, stated that 'there is considerable cross-party agreement on the need for substantial increases, and this remains a priority of the Group's work'. With over a hundred members drawn from all three major parties, the Group has consistently tabled questions on the 'incomes of different groups of pensioners, and called repeatedly for the pension to be increased' (Annual Report, 1992). The Group claims credit, along with the NPC, for the decision to withdraw the increase in VAT on fuel in November 1994.

The House of Lords All Party Group on Ageing, referring to the successful campaign that led to the government's being defeated in its proposal to raise VAT on fuel, stated in its 1994 Annual Report that 'the resulting vote was a tremendous demonstration of the power and influence that older people can exert'. The same report went on to say that older people 'have considerable public sympathy, enormous experience and, once roused, are one of the most formidable lobbying bodies in the country'. This would certainly be true of the early 1940s, the era of the Beveridge Report, and probably the mid-1990s. Neither period can be said, however, to have produced conclusive evidence of the power and influence of older people, only of concerted agitation on the part of pensioners. This suggests that the gap that traditionally exists between 'the great inside and the great outside' remains (Sampson, 1971:3). Access to the 'corridors upstairs', that is, the committee rooms, does not equate with access to the 'corridors of power'. Unhappily for those who seek to voice the demands made by the pensioners' movement on both sides of the House of Commons, and in the House of Lords, sympathy does not necessarily translate into influence where it matters. There are a number of mechanisms by which the voices of older people can be articulated in Parliament and in government, and some new ones have been created; however, being heard is not the same as being listened to. Being consulted does not necessarily mean having power and influencing decisions.

Government Initiatives

There are a number of groups and institutions within the machinery of Parliament and government that take the role of representing or expressing the interests of older people. These have expanded and formalised in recent years, and several initiatives, whose overt purpose is aimed at articulating the voice of older people to government, have been taken. New Labour has clearly acknowledged the presence of an ageing population. In their policy document 'Building a Better Britain for Older People' (DSS, 1998) Tony Blair acknowledged that 'in the past older people have felt that they receive too little attention; their contribution is under valued; and their voices ignored'. Labour's 1997 election manifesto promised a Minister for Older People. This idea was, however, dropped in favour of an 'Inter-Ministerial Group' (IMG). This IMG was chaired by John Denham, the then Minister for Pensions and Social Security, and consisted of 'key' members of each government department, whose brief was to:

> meet to discuss and compare our approaches; to draw on each other's experience to ensure that in each area of government we are responding appropriately to older people ... we have commissioned wide ranging research on older people's attitudes and aspirations. We are also gathering quantified information and statistics. This will all help us paint a better picture of older people's lives and their expectations. (John Denham, speech to the Help the Aged – 'A Life Worth Living' Conference, 13 November 1998)

The initiative produced some important research. In October 1998 the Minister for the Cabinet Office, Dr Jack Cunningham, published the results of the first wave of research by the People's Panel. This panel, which was hailed as 'the world's first national panel, set up to provide a cross-public sector research resource into the effectiveness of government services' (Cabinet Office press release, 29 October 1998) was run by MORI. The panel was a nationally representative sample of people whose opinions on government services could be monitored on a continuing basis. The need to address older people as a specific group was emphasised in the resulting Public Management and Policy Association Lecture, 'Do People's Panels Represent the People?' (17 March 1999). In addition, a new unit within the Cabinet Office, the Performance and Innovation Unit, was given the brief to look at 'active ageing', focusing on ways of 'improving the quality of life of older people' (DSS, 1998:4). These developments effectively set the scene for the further Cabinet Office-initiated research into the attitudes and preoccupations of older people by means of the BGOP programme.

Better Government for Older People

New Labour set out to modernise local government, as part of its general government programme of renewal and reform. Older people were recognised as a relevant part of this process, in part due to an influential report by Professor John Benington of the Warwick University Local Authorities Research Consortium, published in 1996. Benington's report recommended local authority strategies for responding to an ageing population. These recommendations were substantially taken up by New Labour in June 1998 and the BGOP initiative was organised. The Better Government programme was 'a national action-research programme to develop, test, monitor and evaluate integrated, inter-agency strategies and services for an ageing population' (Benington, 1996).

The project was steered by a consortium, led by the Cabinet Office, consisting of the Warwick Working Group on Ageing, Age Concern, the Carnegie Third Age Programme, Anchor Housing and Help the Aged. With well over three hundred organisations involved, it was able to raise interest across the country, and to enlist the cooperation of local government officials in twenty-eight different 'pilot' projects throughout England, Wales, Scotland and Northern Ireland. 'The local pilots ... are developing and testing integrated inter-agency strategies, and examining new and innovative ways of delivering services in ways that promote better co-ordination and responsiveness to users' (BGOP Annual Report, 1998-1999:3). The programme has also set up a Learning Network, which provides a range of services, including an interactive website, a database of good practice, regular bulletins on developments across the programme, and information about workshops.

The involvement of the major charities ensured that the programme would be supported by the most informed and articulate representatives of the voluntary sector, who saw in it evidence of an exciting new attitude towards older people:

> I think that we are at the beginning of nothing less than a revolution in our attitudes to older people, and that means that we must think on a broad canvas, and question ourselves about assumptions, and above all to engage with older people around the country ... to help us to develop this agenda... (Tessa Harding, Head of Planning and Development, Help the Aged, OPPOL interview)

One of the largest of the twenty-eight programme pilots that were running in 2000 is that initiated by Devon County Council. It is a complex pilot, but its overarching objective is a concerted effort on the part of the County Council to improve services to older people and to offer them a say in local government. The project has facilitated the contribution of older people to a wide range of community projects. Central to the understanding of older people's needs and aspirations in the county are the Advisory Group of Older People, consisting of people drawn from seven out of eight District Council areas. As members of Advisory Groups, older people are able to contribute to the debate on how to provide services for older people – 'citizen-centred services' – and to 'develop options for the County Council on the strategic engagement of older people in the long term' (BGOP Annual Report, 1998-1999:35). In terms of Benington's original conception, they are acting as members of a 'community of interest' (Benington, 1996), and constitute a potentially influential voice:

> The new fora that are being developed across the programme are test-beds,

not just for improving services now and in the short term, but experimentation in a new form of local democracy that could shape all our futures. (Martin Shreeve, Programme Director, BGOP, OPPOL)

There are, however, various problems with the way these groups operate, and their purpose is questioned by activists who have experience of working within the pensioners' movement:

Below the Inter-Ministerial Group, the proposed network of Senior Citizen Forums and the National Older People's Advocacy Alliance may well be 'talking shops' with no unity and little lobbying strength. *(Wales Pensioner* (3), Summer 1999:4)

The programme is prepared to challenge government policy, albeit indirectly. For example, BGOP's *Making it Happen, Briefing 2* (Winter 1999/2000) suggests that their programme can 'facilitate older people to set their own agenda in challenging the Pensions Green Paper on the grounds of social inclusion and raising the awareness of younger people of what they will face in retirement'. The same report also suggests that action should be taken to lobby for anti-age discrimination legislation. However, the key focus of BGOP is local government and the services it provides. These events can be influential locally, but there must be some doubt about their ability to influence national policy and sway the balance of political interests at Westminster.

These Labour-initiated administrative reforms and listening programmes directed towards older people can be characterised as consultation exercises rather than as participation in government. There is an effort to consult older people at both a national and local level that is government- and agency-led with many examples of provision of services having been made more responsive and user-friendly at the margins as a result. Thus, such initiatives have their value, but in the context of the future of health and welfare in the new millennium they do not constitute a major reform. What these initiatives do not do is give back citizenship rights as an effective route to healthcare and welfare services (cf. Pickard, 1998). They are part of a management tool intended to target government resources more effectively and keep socially divisive problems at bay. A similar critique is presented by Higgs (1998), who stresses that the role of such exercises is surveillance, better identification of risks, but absolving government from taking active responsibility for the individual consequences of those risks.

6 The Influence of Older Voters – The Case of the 1997 General Election

Introduction

What effect has the ageing population had on electoral politics? There is a range of data that we can call on to examine the significance of increasing numbers of older voters. These include data collected by the research team on the General Election campaign of 1997. There are survey data from a variety of sources, including the British Election Survey (BES) and other attempts to survey the public's response to the election campaign and to document the impact of party political activity on voters. There are academic sources documenting political scientists' assessment of the election and its significance. Newspapers reported daily on the campaign; most broadsheet newspapers are accessible via CD-ROM and thus amenable to qualitative textual analysis. Other archive sources include campaign literature, most importantly the manifestos of the competing parties. It is also possible to ask the general public through focus groups and interviews about their experience of elections. Further it is possible to interview politicians and other participants in the election campaign about their aims, objectives and activities. The research team has drawn on all these sources for this chapter. We have attempted to build a rounded, qualitatively rich picture of the role of older people in the most significant event of British party politics in the last twenty years.

The Main Features of the Campaign

At the start of the 1997 campaign, Labour were already leading in the opinion polls. They had been well ahead for most of the previous four years but were haunted by their last-minute election failure in 1992, which the polls had not foreseen. They therefore conducted a defensive electoral strategy. Their managers' main objective was to 'keep their noses clean'. They sought to avoid saying or doing anything dangerous or controversial that might lose votes. In particular they promoted 'New Labour' with the intention of keeping 'middle England' on board – especially former Conservative voters in key marginal seats who had come across directly to Labour and not to the Liberal Democrats. The key message to these people was caution and financial rectitude.

In contrast, the Conservatives' strategy had to bring them from behind in the polls and attract voters to overcome the Labour lead. They sought to show that there was still a radical New Right vision, that there was still dynamism in 'enterprise culture'. They had to attempt to nullify several image problems acquired by a long period of unpopular government. Their problems can be seen in our interview with an expert election observer:

> And you could track that back to 1992 and Black Wednesday when a lot of the elderly population who are the savers in the population lost a bit of confidence in the Conservative government ... And also the Conservatives' decision to put VAT on domestic fuel, which stirred up a lot of the pensioner population ... just looking at the surveys as they came through, the day-to-day ones, you could see that there was this movement towards the Labour party. (Mervyn Kohler, Head of Public Affairs, Help the Aged, OPPOL interview)

In addition the Conservatives had to combat the tarnish of 'sleaze', and to keep the party's divisions over Europe in check. Their major line of attack was to attempt to reawaken fear of 'old Labour' to undermine New Labour, and to undermine the popular image of Tony Blair by suggesting a hidden left-wing agenda.

Table 6.1 Party votes in 1997 General Election by percentage of age group

Age Group	Did not vote	Conservative	Labour	Liberal Democrat
18-25	29.7	16.8	36.0	14.1
26-35	26.7	17.9	37.6	13.5
36-45	18.9	20.6	39.8	14.8
46-55	15.2	22.8	41.2	14.0
56-65	10.5	27.7	41.7	11.9
66-75	10.1	27.8	43.3	11.8
76 and over	15.8	35.0	26.3	17.3
All ages	18.6	22.8	39.0	13.7

Note: The percentages do not sum to 100% across the rows, as the Nationalists and minor parties and those who refused to disclose their vote are not included.
Source: Authors' analysis of 1997 BES.

In the event, the Conservatives failed to recapture defectors to New Labour. The result of the British 1997 General Election was to remove the Conservative government from office and leave the Labour Party dominating the House of Commons with a 178-seat majority. The distribution of voters between the major parties and the pattern of voting by age is illustrated in Table 6.1. The age group with the lowest percentage of Labour voters was the oldest.

Preparation and planning are vital to electoral success (and such plans reveal the priorities of parties in terms of target value given to certain kinds of voters, such as older people). Party political election campaigns make use of the media and try to control the 'agenda' in systematic pre-planned ways. The principle targets for the parties' campaigns in the 1997 election were key groups of voters in marginal seats and were defined in terms of party allegiance and salience of issues. Geographical targeting, that is, selection of priority areas, took place.

> Well, the target campaign, organised in 1992, was directing anything of help you could towards those seats which you had a greater prospect of winning or which you felt were particularly vulnerable. And these resources consisted of, in part, finance – but that was a small part, – in part, professional advice – that was a large part. I had a small team of people giving very in-depth guidance to particular constituencies. In part it was rationing the leader's time, so that in the run-up to the campaign and during it the leader and the other MPs were particularly busy with these seats. (A party campaign manager, OPPOL interview)

Targeting also took place in terms of selection of issues. Identifying which issue would influence different types of voters was also part of the strategy in selecting ways to attack and defend. Older people have particular interests and are concerned about some issues above others.

> Pensions was a topical issue during the campaign, yes, with the scare story about the Conservatives abolishing the state pension. But I would say that in the polling that we did, that pensioners, as well as being concerned about the pensions, were particularly concerned about crime and about health. And we were majoring very much on the Health Service, and we thought that had particular appeal to older people. (A party campaign manager, OPPOL interview)

The extent to which older people's issues were targeted and addressed during the campaign can be viewed from a range of sources, for example, the way issues were reported through the media. There are obvious routines by which the political parties feed information to the media. Press conferences were a daily ritual during the General Election.

Photo opportunities were engineered by the politicians to meet the continuous demand for visual and televisual images from the media. This necessitated forward planning, and although the best-laid plans can go awry, the parties' election campaigns were prepared so that the issues and the images that play best for each of them were sequentially delivered for the attention of voters via the media.

> What to do next: x-number of days on health, x-number on education and x-number of days on crime, so that we had a fixed plan which involved a press conference in the morning dealing with that issue, and then [the leader] going on tour and being part of a photo connected with that issue ... If you note that things have changed in a certain way you are inclined to say, ok, we'll do one more press conference on this, one less on that, but largely we stuck to our battle plan. (A party campaign manager, OPPOL interview)

However, flexibility and the ability to respond to a changing agenda are also a requisite for politicians reliant on the media to communicate with voters. Labour's rapid rebuttal techniques, which they developed as the result of mistakes in the 1992 election, and from close observation of the American Presidential elections, were very effective. They fed the media's desire for controversy and rapid, constantly changing text. They had a prepared database from which media watchers could instantaneously call up effective responses to adverse comment, enabling them to 'spin' issues in ways that suited their strategy.

Thus a crucial electoral battleground was the struggle to have issues placed on the public agenda and, for example, discussed in the media. The issues that most directly affected older people as an interest group in the election were issues of poverty, pensions and residential care. Groups representing older people succeeded in getting these at least partially on the agenda. For example the *Guardian* used Age Concern material to produce the following quotations:

> We have more elderly people than ever before in this country. There are 10.6 million pensioners and most are short of cash. Two thirds of pensioner households are below the threshold for income tax. The state pension was aligned with prices and the link broken with incomes in the early years of the Thatcher government. The purchasing power of the pension has effectively not risen since nineteen eighty...If the politicians gloss over pensions and the long-term care of the elderly – 40,000 are having to sell their homes each year to pay for residential care – they can focus on general health service or education issues, in which older people express a keen interest. (*Guardian*, 18 April 1997, quoting Mervyn Kohler, Head of Public Affairs, Help the Aged)

As its Director General, Sally Greengross felt that Age Concern has over the years had an effect during elections, specifically during the 1997 election campaign, when Age Concern identified and raised issues through its own manifesto. She indicates the main agenda-setting tools in the following terms:

> Nationally, in early 1997 we published a manifesto, *Age Matters*, which was publicly available and circulated to all candidates of major parties standing in the General Election. The manifesto was handed in to each party headquarters at a photo-launch in Westminster with an ad-mobile showing a photo of an older man with the strapline 'Your Vote Counts'. The ad-mobile toured the nation for one week in February 1997.
>
> In addition, we published a survey showing how many older voters there are in each Parliamentary constituency to reinforce the point about the electoral power of older voters (the national average is 24% of electorate over state pension age and 58% of the electorate over 40; almost 50% of the electorate is aged over 45). This received considerable local, regional and national coverage.
>
> We also conducted a Gallup survey in April 1996 to gauge people's views on the key issues to help us prepare our manifesto.
>
> Locally and regionally, Age Concern groups promoted the issues in the manifesto. Age Concern England held a number of regional seminars to assist them between September 1996 and early 1997. Also, we published an A4 card entitled 'Your Vote Counts' summarising the key issues and how to register to vote for circulation to older people themselves. Thousands were circulated.
>
> At the Autumn 1996 party conferences we took exhibition space at the three main conferences with a stand illustrating the older voter and with constituency material to again press home the point about the electoral power of older voters and their high turnout rate. We also held fringe meetings on the broad theme of what older people expect from each political party. (Sally Greengross, Director General, Age Concern, OPPOL interview)

The Pensions Issue

One possible way to look at the importance of older people in the electoral process is to look at the way in which the issues that concern them most were treated. The major issue for older people was pensions. The Labour manifesto stated:

> We believe that all pensioners should share fairly in the increasing prosperity of the nation. Instead of privatisation, we propose a partnership between public and private provision, and a balance between income sourced from tax and invested savings. The basic state pension will be retained as the foundation of pension provision. It will be increased at least

in line with prices. We will examine means of delivering more automatic help to the poorest pensioners – one million of whom do not even receive the Income Support which is their present entitlement...

...Too many people in work, particularly those on low and modest incomes and with changing patterns of employment, cannot join good-value second pension schemes. Labour will create a new framework – stakeholder pensions – to meet this need. We will encourage new partnerships between financial service companies, employers and employees to develop these pension schemes. They will be approved to receive people's savings only if they meet high standards of value for money, flexibility and security...

...We will also seek to develop the administrative structure of SERPS [State Earnings Related Pension Scheme] so as to create a 'citizenship pension' for those who assume responsibility as carers, as a result lose out on the pension entitlements they would otherwise acquire, and currently end up on means-tested benefits. (Labour Party Manifesto, 1997)

These high-sounding ideals are in fact a change from Labour's previous commitments. Colin Hay (1999:120) suggests that this is:

perhaps the single most significant revision to Labour's welfare policy in recent years. Where the party was, in 1992, committed to the effective restoration of earnings-linked public pensions, it approached the 1997 general election with no proposals to modify the Conservatives' price-indexation formula.

Given that the history of 'pension reform' over the last twelve years focused on reducing benefits, it is not surprising that there was widespread pessimism about future provision. The *Times* reported that '8 out of 10 voters questioned expected the state pension to be phased out regardless of which party wins the election' (*Times*, 27 April 1997, 'In the Gutter' feature, Grice et al.).

This pessimism about the state pension gave the Conservatives the chance to gain an initiative, and they brought out major new proposals for pension reform during the election. Perhaps they were trying to show the continued reforming nature of their neo-liberal economic approach. Perhaps they were even trying to draw on their previous reputation for financial management and fiscal rectitude. However, they did not manage to pull it off and the initiative backfired. This is a verbatim transcript of the Deputy Leader of the Conservative Party presenting their policies in a televised debate:

Increasingly a very large number of our people are now in occupational pension schemes, through companies or whatever it may be and they're funded and they get something like a half to two-thirds of their income, last year's income, on retirement. And that leaves a gap between those who only have the State Pension. Now the taxpayer can't afford to increase the State Pension to match what's happening in the private sector – everyone knows that – overnight. But we've looked ahead to this generation and we've said that we will start – probably in about four years' time – we will start to create for everybody their own investment scheme which will be funded every year by contributions based on their National Insurance scheme. So that when they retire, when he retires, sometime towards the middle of the next century, he will have accumulated a fund which will have been invested on his behalf, all through those forty years and it – our calculations – the government's actuary, it's not a politician, the government's actuary calculations – are that by the time he retires, this fund could have delivered him a Pension which would be worth about a hundred and seventy-five pounds a week compared with the present State Pension. But the guarantee is there that whatever the result of the investments that will be made on his behalf, the basic standard State Pension, inflation proof, will remain a guarantee right the way through ... So that's a radical attempt to deal with the problem of an ageing population and we're the only Party that's had the courage to say that. (Michael Heseltine in the televised Deputy Leaders debate during the 1997 campaign, BBC transcript)

Labour was able to exploit fears about the pension and launched an immediate counter-attack. They suggested that the Conservatives would privatise the pension.

Gordon Brown, the Shadow Chancellor, said it was a known fact that the 'Conservative plan is to abolish the state pension, replacing the basic state pension with privately purchased provision'. He also queried the suggestion in the proposals that 'it might be possible to bring older people into the scheme at a later date if public finances permitted'. (*Times*, 26 April 1997, 'The battle switches to the cost of pensions', Sherman and Kennedy)

This accusation was of course resented and challenged by John Major and the Conservatives.

His irritation at Labour's line of attack was all the greater because he grew up in a family where hardship was no stranger, with a sick, elderly father, an unwell mother and only two rooms to live in. He threw Blair's pensions charges back in his teeth in the most emotional rebuttal of his entire career in politics at an unscheduled meeting with reporters during a factory visit in Newcastle upon Tyne. (*Times*, 27 April 1997, 'In the Gutter' feature, Grice et al.)

This response also has to be understood in the context of John Major's attempts to build on his image as a trusted man of the people in touch with ordinary experiences and voters, a necessary strategy given his relatively greater popularity compared to that of his party.

It is ironic that the Conservatives sought to use the issue of pensions to show that they had not run out of ideas and to appeal to younger people. The Conservatives, it is suggested, used the issue to show a continued momentum to their radical, New Right reforms (Jones, 1997:246). Indeed the Conservative manifesto refers to the increasing proportion of older people in the population, not to appeal for their votes, but rather to suggest a looming crisis that would affect younger people and which their initiative was set to address. The Tories were reported as being 'serious here to help young people have a proper pension' (*Guardian*, 26 April 1997, 'Think of Mawhinney smiling, vote Labour', Hardy).

However, Labour turned the initiative by concentrating on older people. Much of Labour's attack hinged on the White Paper's phrase that 'it might be possible to bring older people into the scheme at a later date if public finances permitted'. Labour were brazen and unrepentant about raising fears about the pension. They are reported as having used such fears to powerful effect in personal contact with voters.

> If elderly people, used to collecting their pensions weekly at the post office, thought their entitlement would be put at risk by another five years of Tory power, so be it. 'If that's how people choose to read it...' said a Labour official. (*Times*, 27 April 1997, 'In the Gutter' feature, Grice et al.)

There were some qualms amongst the Labour ranks about the potential anxiety and distress that raising distorted fears might generate for older people. A point that the Tories, of course, also made.

> A Labour candidate, probably to be made a Minister in a Labour government, was out canvassing on Friday when she got into conversation with an elderly lady who burst into tears out of fear that the Conservatives will abolish the state pension. The easy reaction would have been a homily on the government's wickedness and a pointed reminder to vote Labour on Thursday. Instead, the candidate – who has asked not to be identified – felt moved to explain the government's Basic Pension Plan proposal, to assure the old lady that not even the Conservatives would be so heartless as to leave her destitute. She said afterwards: 'I do feel slightly squeamish about the pensions thing. It has been an incredibly powerful message, which on an individual basis has created a lot of fear. It's part of a major political strategy which has a highly personal impact. We have won it hands down. The Tories are completely on the back foot. (The *Observer*, 27 April 1997, 'Final round polls apart as pensions spark an age-old battle of shouting

"Liar!"', Wintur and McSmith)

There was a further risk that the negative attack could backfire. There was a chance that the 'tax and spend' label might reattach itself to Labour. Labour felt the need to cultivate an image of financial prudence and give no financial hostages to fortune about extra expenditure. This meant that they backtracked on previous pension commitments and limited their pronouncements to generalities about pensioners being better off under Labour. The problem of this position was illustrated by Grice and colleagues in the *Times*. They report on the Labour leader's participation in exchanges with a television audience on the issue. On 'Question Time' Tony Blair warned of 'two-tier' pensions under the Conservatives but was challenged by Roy Allison, a retired Methodist minister from Devon, to radically review the way state pensions are calculated.

> 'Well, Roy, I've got to try and operate within the situation that I'll inherit,' Blair replied. 'I mean, all these things come in the end down to pounds, shillings and pence. And, you know, there are a lot of calls on government and government finances and we've got to take all those things into account.' Challenged by Allison's persistent questioning, Blair refused to budge, aware of the damage previous Labour leaders have suffered when they made expensive promises. 'I've said to you I will do my best by Britain's pensioners as previous Labour governments have done, but I'm not going to make any promises to you that I can't keep,' said Blair. (*Times*, 27 April 1997, 'In the Gutter' feature, Grice et al.)

On social issues more generally Labour had a reputation as a party that gave a higher priority to public services and supporting the vulnerable than its main rivals did. Negative campaigning on this topic, however, proved very effective for Labour. Labour used negative advertising on television to warn voters of the dangers of another Tory five-year term. These adverts were reported in the *Times*, which noted that among the warnings were pictures of patients on trolleys in hospital corridors, elderly residents in a nursing home, vandalism and juvenile crime, together with:

> stark written messages: '50,000 fewer nurses ... The Tories are pulling the NHS apart. The Tories will sell off old people's homes ... Crime has doubled under the Tories'. (*Times*, 21 April 1997, 'Broadcast invokes Elgar to undermine the Tories', Sherman)

These concerns resonate with older people. The tone of the paper's comment is somewhat cynical and distanced but acknowledges the power of the broadcast. One of Labour strategies was to maximise its advantage as being seen as the party most likely to support health and welfare agendas and it sought to do so through this broadcast. However, it is not clear (indeed it is unlikely) that they were specifically trying to appeal to an older audience. They were appealing to the 'compassionate' ageism[22] of the general population, who feel that government should make sure older people are cared for, nursed and not victims of crime. Indeed all voters have an interest in pension provision, although that interest is neither held in common nor completely transparent to those whose interests are affected.

The burden of this discussion of how old-age issues featured in the media during the 1997 election campaign suggests strongly that the battle was not over the votes of older people *per se*. The party campaigners selected issues to promote but did not choose them because they would be specifically attractive to older people. Pensions were an important issue, but it was not that the party campaigners saw older people as a priority group whose votes they had to attract. Rather, they were seeking to position their parties so that they could portray them as the guardians of 'compassionate ageism' and the other parties as insincere and not to be trusted on pensions and old-age issues. The problem for Labour was to use this issue without making themselves vulnerable to the accusation of being a party of high spending. The problem for the Tories was how to appear compassionate while generating a progressive image through a radical free-market policy reform of welfare. The media commentators themselves did not see old-age issues as being decisive or seek to analyse the election in terms of age-based interests.

Older People as Targets for Political Campaigns

The response of party politicians and organisers to demographic change appears to have been limited. Evidence from key figures suggested they did not think in such terms. Party political strategies did not seek to target seats on the basis of age profiles. Some activists argue that the only responses to the increased numbers of older voters have been cosmetic, cosmetic in the sense that they are more to do with presentation than with the substance of policies or the priority given to older people's interests. For example, the media campaigns may have changed to include images on posters or in broadcasts that depicted respected and respectable older people. A campaigns manager for the Liberal Democrats said, 'Our manifesto, ... we have pictures of people on the front, and we have a balanced range of people between young and old in the photographs'.

Candidates and party workers in their training may be taught methods of communication, including ways of talking to or approaching

---

[22] See Chapter 8 for a discussion of compassionate ageism.

older people. The election teams may have carefully briefed candidates on how to respond to pressure-group questionnaires, including advice on ways to deal with older people and their issues. But these activities were not central to the campaign and not crucial to the result. Those committed to older people's causes, including politicians, see a cynicism in the neglect of older voters.

> But you know people write to me angry with the way that they are treated and the attitude that the government has to them that they really are people to be patted on the head. 'Go away, you're not going to last very long anyway' and the people you want to look after are young people because they're going to be voting for the next forty years. There is a cynicism from politicians on elderly people. (Paul Flynn, Labour Party MP, OPPOL interview)

The parties' electoral strategists use opinion polling and focus groups to keep track of opinions. Party strategists we talked to had an awareness of the changing demographic realities and conduct market research to understand the age segmentation of the electorate. One said:

> We're always doing market research, we'll always do some groups of older people. We particularly noticed, since the general election, about the pensions issue. We noted that older people continue to be more concerned with health and crime than younger people do, and we'll continue to look at them. (OPPOL interview)

Although Sally Greengross suggested that parties were sensitive to older voters, she also commented that 'all parties appeared to underestimate the electoral power of older people and their high turnout rates'. It should not be unexpected that those who are seeking to lobby politicians in the interests of older people suggest that they are important electorally. However, there is much evidence to suggest that it is reasonably unlikely that Labour was specifically targeting older voters. For example, there was the revelation by the Tories during the last days of the campaign of Labour's 'battlebook', containing its alleged strategy for the campaign. The suggested electoral targets in this document did not include older people. Five target groups were specified:

> These are: swing voters, characterised as typically mortgage holders, younger people on higher incomes; women, especially the twenty-five to forty age group who are nervous about change and about Labour and who like Major's decency and honesty; first-time voters, who are less likely to vote than their elders and are concerned about money and jobs; the DEs [social class designations] – unskilled and unemployed manual workers

who have a low propensity to vote and tend to ask what's in it for them; and, finally, voters in the fifteen seats in the crucial Pennine Belt, who are unusually suspicious of Labour and who cast their votes on the basis of economic self-interest and confidence. (*Guardian*, 24 April 1997, 'The election: Labour's plan of attack', Kettle)

Insofar as 'first-time' voters were targeted, this suggests Labour was more interested in young voters than in older ones.

I remember we went to Mandelson[23] at the party conference in Blackpool and talked it through with him and said 'look, these are very key issues', because he kept saying, you know, 'New Labour, Young Labour, New Britain, Young Britain', it's all very very youth orientated. Mandelson turned around and said to us, 'Well you're absolutely right, I'm just not interested in older voters because they don't change their vote'. (Lobbyist for Age Concern, OPPOL interview)

However, the lobbyist felt that they had some success by being able to call on alternative psephological information. He felt he might have influenced the Labour 'scare on pensions' line of attack.

And we actually had some research that said they might change their vote they weren't as solid as he [Mandelson] thought they were. An interesting thing was, in the run-up to the election, he suddenly did this whole thing on pensions. It was a scary number about what the Tories were going to do to pensions. (OPPOL interview)

Again, this is a charity campaigner who has an interest in suggesting that the votes of older people were there to be won. Media sources quote Labour campaigners as reportedly thinking that the pensions issue was:

'a great issue'. One Labour strategist explained why: 'Our biggest problem group is women over fifty-five. This helps us in our weakest spot. We have started to close that gap'. (*Times*, 27 April 1997, 'In the Gutter' feature, Grice et al.)

Political parties do regular opinion polling. It is well established that older people typically have a greater propensity to vote, and have historically tended to vote in greater proportions for the Conservatives than other parties. The key issue was then the extent to which older people were likely to switch their votes. The power of the grey vote is diminished if

---

[23] Peter Mandelson, Labour MP and subsequently minister, who is credited with creating the New Labour image and masterminding their successful 1997 election campaign.

election strategists believe that older people do not change their votes. In 2000, with Labour planning for the next election, the *Times* castigated what it called 'Category Politics'. In this piece Labour planners are condemned for what they have denied saying, on the basis that many people would believe they said it, and that the opinions are nevertheless accurate!

> It is arrogant to write off large sections of voters. Deny them as they may, tales told of politicians can be deadlier than the truth when the purported comments ring true with voters. Peter Mandelson may never have told a Millbank meeting of Labour's general election planning committee that there is 'no mileage' to be had from pensioners, or that Labour should fix its sights on Britain's 'aspirational voters'. But the words fit with his public image. Perish the thought that Clive Soley, the Labour Party chairman, would ever have muttered that pensioners are 'predominantly Conservative' – which is true, on their voting record – let alone that he classed as racist their complaints, which he admits receiving in the piled mailbags, expressing outrage that the basic pension is to rise by only 75p a week, that the government devotes more time and money to asylum-seekers than to the elderly. But the thought will not perish. (*Times*, 17 April 2000)

Party organisers did not feel that older people would switch votes to the same extent as younger voters would. When interviewed, one campaign manager said:

> I think in a way one of the things that probably undermines the power of older people as a voting group is that the older you are the less likely you are to change your vote and therefore people probably realise that the number of votes that are up for grabs among that group are not as great as they are in other groups. (OPPOL interview)

Another campaign manager from a different party analysed the older vote in the following terms:

> The key kind of point about the age pattern of the electorate is that the older the age group, the less likely they are to be swing voters and also the more likely they are to vote. Historically, the older age group, certainly those over the age of 55, are very, very much more Conservative than the rest of the population. In fact, you could say that of the core Conservative vote at the moment the vast bulk of it is aged over 55. The exit poll had us neck and neck amongst pensioners, whereas [Labour] were three to one ahead amongst people under the age of 35. It's one of the big kind of sociological issues, whether people become more conservative as they grow older or whether you're talking about particular cohorts within the population that might have particular characteristics. It's probably more a

product of the kind of demography of it that basically working-class people don't live as long as middle-class people, so that means that there is in that oldest age group social imbalance and a gender imbalance as well, which builds it up. Historically, because [Labour] have been a trade unionist, manufacturing, working-class party, their strongest base of support has tended to be more amongst men than amongst women. (OPPOL interview)

It is possible to look at independent evidence at to the character of the older vote. Evidence of the 1997 British Election Survey (BES) can be used to try to identify the extent to which older people had a different

Table 6.2 Change in strength of intention to vote Labour between 2nd and 3rd waves of 1997 BES panel study

Age Group	Weaker intention to vote Labour	No change	Stronger intention to vote Labour	Total
17-24	22	264	41	327
	6.70%	80.70%	12.60%	100.00%
25-34	68	600	82	750
	9.10%	80.00%	11.00%	100.00%
35-44	52	528	79	659
	7.90%	80.10%	11.90%	100.00%
45-54	44	492	66	602
	7.30%	81.70%	11.00%	100.00%
55-59	22	185	23	230
	9.60%	80.40%	10.00%	100.00%
60-64	20	178	23	221
	9.00%	80.50%	10.40%	100.00%
65+	62	712	84	858
	7.20%	83.00%	9.80%	100.00%
DK/Refused/ Not answered	–	14	1	15
	–	93.30%	6.70%	100.00%
Total	290	2973	399	3662
	7.90%	81.20%	10.90%	100.00%

Source: Authors' analysis of the 1997 BES.

propensity to change their vote than younger people did. The BES conducted a panel study to trace changes in voting intention during the election campaign, measuring the strength of intention to vote for particular parties on a ten-point scale. Tables 6.2 and 6.3 summarise the data indicating any changes of intensity of feeling towards Labour and the Conservatives respectively.

The tables suggest that there was some evidence that older people, those over 55, were less likely to change their vote than younger age groups were, but if they did, they were more likely to change in a rightward direction than were the rest of the population. Of the '65 and over' age group, 83% did not change their attitude to Labour and fewer of this group

Table 6.3 Change in strength of intention to vote Conservative between 2nd and 3rd waves of 1997 BES panel study

Age Group	Weaker intention to vote Conservative	No change	Stronger intention to vote Conservative	Total
17-24	49	212	66	327
	15.0%	64.8%	20.2%	100.0%
25-34	100	491	159	750
	13.3%	65.5%	21.2%	100.0%
35-44	89	448	122	659
	13.5%	68.0%	18.5%	100.0%
45-54	85	406	111	602
	14.1%	67.4%	18.4%	100.0%
55-59	31	166	33	230
	13.5%	72.2%	14.3%	100.0%
60-64	24	169	28	221
	10.9%	76.5%	12.7%	100.0%
65+	119	645	94	858
	13.9%	75.2%	11.0%	100.0%
DK/Refused/ Not answered	–	15	–	15
	–	100.0%	–	100.0%
Total	497	2552	613	3662
	13.6%	69.7%	16.7%	100.0%

Source: Authors' analysis of the 1997 BES.

moved *towards* Labour than in any other age category. Eleven percent of the sample aged 65 and over moved away from the Conservatives, fewer

than in any other age group and 75.2% did not change their attitude towards
the Conservatives; only the 60-64-year-old group was less likely to change.
But although these tables indicate a general trend not to change parties as
readily as other age groups do, this tendency is far from a universal
characteristic among older people.

Do Local Party Campaigns Target Pensioners?

In our interviews with party election organisers at a national level, most

Table 6.4 Targets for local leaflet campaigns

Target group	No. of targeted leaflets	% of leaflets targeted
First-time Voters	324	23.60
Rivals' Supporters	154	11.22
Own Supporters	93	6.77
Undecided	93	6.77
Postal Voters	51	3.71
Local Election	19	1.38
Pensioners	133	9.69
Ethnic Minorities	67	4.88
Parents	57	4.15
Farmers	44	3.20
Businesses	30	2.18
Specific Occupational Groups	30	2.18
Council Tenants	19	1.38
Women	14	1.02
Animal Lovers	12	0.87
Commuters	11	0.80
Home Owners	3	0.22
Unemployed	2	0.15
Church Groups	1	0.07
Other	216	15.73
Total	1373	100.00

Source: Authors' analysis of Denver, D. T. and Hands, G., 'Constituency Campaigning in
the 1997 General Election' (computer file), Colchester, Essex: The Data Archive
(distributor), 17 August 1999, SN: 3922.

said they felt that targeting seats and voters was more important than
targeting age or socio-economic groups.

> Yes, we concentrated much more heavily on the target seat operation in
> '97 than '92. We did much less in terms of national newspaper

advertising. (Party campaign manager)

Less? (Interviewer)

Less in '97, less national newspaper advertising in '97 than '92, but more support to the constituencies to help pay for organisers and things like that. (Party campaign manager, OPPOL interview)

It is possible to ask to what extent local parties campaigning in their constituencies saw older voters as an important group to target.

Denver and Hands (1999) carried out a survey of party agents after the 1997 General Election. They found that, of the 1,382 campaign officials who responded, 56.1% sent targeted leaflets, some of whom sent multiple target leaflets. First-time voters were by far the most common target for leaflets (accounting for 23.6% of the total number of leaflets). These voters are easy to identify because the electoral register records the birthday of those who are 18 during the time the register is in force. These voters are sent birthday cards and similar items to encourage them not only to vote for the party concerned, but also to gain their interest in voting. The other target groups were very diverse but each represented only a small proportion of leaflets distributed (see Table 6.4): 11.22% targeted rival supporters, while 9.69% targeted pensioners.

The Response of the Pundits, or The Dog that Didn't Bark

Examination of the major political studies of the 1997 election reveals that the issue of an ageing electorate and its interests is totally absent from their discussions. In the academic sphere, the fifth volume in the series *Developments in British Politics* (Dunleavy et al., 1997), in which leading political science academics discuss the 1997 General Election and what it means in terms of the changing nature of British politics, does not discuss the issue in any of its eighteen sections, nor is the issue raised in the volume in any form whatsoever. Mark Evans discusses 'Political Participation' and has a short section on 'Age' but this is entirely devoted to youth. David Sanders discusses voting and the electorate using survey data that includes tables with distribution of voting patterns by age, but age plays no part in his insightful analysis of the shifting attitudes of different sections of the public to the contending political parties and the roots of the Labour victory. Similarly *Critical Elections* (Evans and Norris, 1999), another work in which leading political scientists try to assess the significance of the 1997 General Election, does not consider the demographic ageing of the electorate as an issue. It contains contributions on 'new social alignments', but these are identified as class, gender, race and region; age is simply not discussed. Similarly, Worcester and Mortimore's discussion *Explaining Labour's Landslide* (1999) contains no comment on an ageing electorate. The point here is not that these analyses are inadequate, but rather that if the leading academic commentators cannot identify an increasingly powerful lobby of older people, it probably doesn't exist, except in the ideological perspective of some interested parties.

Nick Jones provides a view of the 1997 General Election from a journalist's perspective. He gives a blow-by-blow account of the campaign as it happened and the reactions, as he saw them, of the key players to what transpired. He includes analysis of the strategies of the various parties and leaders. Again, issues of old age played no part in the campaign by his analysis, and old age scarcely figures in the book. He does give a detailed account of the closing exchanges on pensions, but does not place this in the context of older voters or an ageing electorate; rather, he uses the story to emphasise the ruthlessness of Labour's propaganda machine (Jones, 1997:242-6).

In both Dunleavy et al. and Jones there is some reference to social policy and to pensions in particular. It is clear that the welfare state and pensions were a significant policy issue discussed in the campaign. What is also clear, however, is that no major political party, nor their leaders or campaign strategists, nor major academic or journalistic commentators on the election considered that the votes of older people had any strategic significance to its outcome. Insofar as pensions were a contentious issue, party initiatives were directed neither exclusively nor even in major form to older people.

The Impact of Age on the Election

Thus older people did not figure as a significant group whose vote the parties identified as key to the election. The most important group of voters by age were 30-50-year-olds. These were people who as younger voters had voted for Thatcher governments in the eighties. There was much discussion of the 'feel-good factor' during the campaign. The section of 'middle England' that is 'middle' by age group had its sense of prosperity dented by difficulties with the housing market – they were hit by mortgage hikes and negative equity. To some extent unemployment, but more importantly increased job insecurity in white-collar occupations, started to trouble this group. They were also concerned about the education of their children. In terms of old-age issues, they were concerned about their own future old age and their parents' current care needs. Their future pensions and old-age provision worried this group as they entered their middle age. They saw their parents' property at risk in paying for long-term care where they might have expected to inherit it. As an above-average income group, but by no means wealthy, they were aware that they could not afford private care. These factors meant that this formerly conservative middle England group had a relatively low feel-good factor despite a relatively good economic prognosis for the country as a whole. In contrast, the more affluent section of the over-60s population, because of occupational pensions, had a relatively high feel-good factor. They were having a significantly better retirement than their parents had. Those older people who were relatively worse off were those relying exclusively on a state pension, and these people were not traditional Tory voters. The battleground of the 1997 election was the floating voters of middle England, who were to some extent the middle-aged as well as the middle-class.

From a wide variety of evidence, it can be concluded that older people were not a key group in the campaign for votes in 1997. However, there is a case that, in more diffuse terms – the public agenda of issues and concerns – the influence of generations may be discernible, and this is taken up in subsequent chapters. The argument that identifies older people as a potentially powerful electoral force makes the mistake of equating biological age with social category. Older people are not a single group but an increasingly diverse set of people. It has been argued that there has been a change in modern society that has led to a decline in the strength of class, gender, national and age identities. The declining significance of age-based occupational and other categories defined by the state and other large-scale organisations means that, although there are now a greater number of older people, they have less unity of interest and less sense of common identity. The significant political change is not the numbers of older voters, but their increasingly diverse interests.

7 The Influence of the Pensioners' Movement – The Issue of the State Pension

Introduction

'The pension' is both symbolically and in practical terms a central element of the welfare state. Together with the National Health Service, the state pension continues to have very large popular support. It is paid at a universal flat rate to all senior citizens by virtue of their National Insurance contributions. The first part of this chapter looks at the development of the 'pensions issue' in a historical context, tracing the erratic course of government pensions policy since 1940, in order to illustrate the essentially political nature of decisions taken by government where pensions are concerned. We then follow the response to government policy of the pensioners' movement, demonstrating the tendency of the movement to adopt the stance of a 'single issue' pressure group, the single issue in question being that of restoring the link with average earnings, which was broken in 1980. At present the basic state pension is only systematically uprated in line with an index of price inflation. For the pensioners' movement the answer is simple: the state scheme must be supported and given an annual boost by being uprated in line with average male earnings. The chapter concludes by reflecting on the opposition the pensioners' movement has faced in mounting its campaign to have the link restored.

A Contemporary History of the Pensions Issue

Pensions in the Post-Second World War Context

An examination of the history of the postwar political debates over the pension can help in the attempt to assess the impact of the pensioners' movement on British politics. The first state pension was created in 1908. The current scheme was developed in the 1940s as part of a series of measures that established the welfare state with a promise of care 'from the cradle to the grave'. The state pension was to provide guaranteed financial security in the last part of the life-course. Britain, along with the rest of the world, experienced a rapidly growing postwar economy that contrasted strongly with the recession of the 1930s. Rising wages increased the popularity of the idea of earnings-related pensions. The 1959 National Insurance Act introduced a graduated scheme. However, the Conservatives placed the emphasis on private pension provision[24] and ensured that the Exchequer would pay less into the scheme than was predicted by the 1946 National Insurance Act (Labour Research, 1958:177, 1959:30). The immediate postwar austerity gave way to relative affluence, but not for all. Despite the fact of 'rising living standards for the pampered majority there was very real hardship for the neglected minority, especially old age pensioners' (Marwick, 1963:140). By 1970 the policy of 'targeting' the poorest pensioners in order that 'help will go where it is most needed'[25] was officially endorsed by the Conservative Chancellor of the Exchequer. However, the issue of means testing, with its association with the discredited welfare regimes of the 1930s, was an anathema to pensioner activists.

Pension Developments Under Labour Governments of the 1970s

The Labour Party's policy on pensions came to place increasing emphasis on relating retirement income more closely to the living standards of the working population. Labour stated in their 1970 manifesto:

> The present national insurance scheme, in spite of the improvements which Labour has made, cannot provide an adequate income for retirement. Flat-rate contribution and benefits must inevitably be geared to the ability of the lowest paid to enter into the insurance contract. As a result, those on average and above average pay would always find a steep drop in their means upon retirement.
> Labour's new Pension Plan will, therefore, incorporate radical concepts in social security; earnings-related contributions will mean a reduction for millions of lower paid workers.

However, Labour lost to the Conservatives under Edward Heath in the 1970 General Election. This deprived Labour of the opportunity to implement plans developed by the former Minister Richard Crossman to reform the pension system. When Labour finally regained power in 1974, Barbara Castle was given the brief to carry forward the reform of pensions.

---

[24] Private pension schemes were, indeed, accounting for roughly half the male employed population (Labour Research, 1959:30).

[25] This is taken from a statement made by the Chancellor of the Exchequer after the Conservative Party's Selsdon Conference, at which the policy agenda for the new Heath government was set.

Thus the two most influential figures in the pensioners' movement in the last fifty years came simultaneously to be in positions of national power – Barbara Castle as a senior cabinet minister and Jack Jones as the most influential leader of the trade union side of the Labour movement.

The trade unions were a significant influence on the Labour governments of the 1970s and they had become more interested in the pensions issue. Earnings-related pensions depended upon a contribution record. Those who were too old or too badly paid to benefit from such schemes have remained amongst the poorest people in Britain. Bornat (1998:189) speaks of 'significant gains' for pensioner organisations at the time. Jack Jones outlined some of the benefits:

> The programme which the Labour Party eventually accepted which they fought the election on ... one part of that was the removal of the Industrial Relations Act, which happened, another part was to increase pensions. The basic national insurance pension was to be lifted by nearly 30%. This was the programme of the very limited, very weak pensioners' movement which I and the TUC had adopted. The proposal was for £16 for a couple and £10 for a single person, but it represented a nearly 30% increase.... (Jack Jones, President of the NPC, OPPOL interview)

The price of trade union support for an anti-inflationary policy of wage restraint in the mid-1970s was an improvement to the 'social wage'. Jack Jones was an important figure in securing that support. The pension improvements were part of the increased collective benefits for working people to compensate for limitations placed on wage increases. In 1975 the Social Security Pensions Act, often referred to as the 'Castle Plan', after Barbara Castle, was passed. Complex and innovative, the plan introduced the State Earnings Related Pension Scheme (SERPS), which based benefits on the best twenty years of earnings and substantially improved women's entitlement. Alongside SERPS, which spread the equivalent of occupational pensions to a large proportion of the working population, the Act required the Secretary of State to 'estimate the general level of earnings and prices in such manner as he thinks fit and ... have regard either to earnings or prices according to which he considers more advantageous to beneficiaries'. In practice this meant that, in years when prices rose faster than earnings, pensions increased in line with the Retail Price Index, and in years when earnings rose faster, they were increased in line with the Average Earnings Index. Enormous gains were made in the period 1974-79, and the pensioners' movement was, if not at the heart of government deliberations on pensions policy, in a position of influence.

The precise involvement of the pensioners' movement is difficult to determine, but narratives of the movement from participants and academics have indicated that its role was significant. However, our informants suggested that Barbara Castle's consultations with the TUC on the legislation were limited. This is hardly surprising given the legacy of her role in the struggles over trade union reform at the end of the Wilson government in the late sixties. 'In Place of Strife', the policy put forward for Wilson by Barbara Castle, was strongly resisted by the trade union movement, including Jack Jones. This clash echoes down the history of the British pensioners' movement even into the twenty-first century. The pensioners' movement alliance with the trade unions did not necessarily place it the centre of policy formulation at this time. As the movement failed to gain credit for the passing of SERPS, its reputation for effectiveness was diminished. However, informed commentators we interviewed on this period suggest that the idea that the government passed the Castle Act without an awareness of public pressure on the pensions issue is implausible. Indeed, one of the dominant ideas in Labour politics of the time was the idea of the 'social wage'. This policy explicitly linked trade union cooperation with government on an anti-inflationary incomes policy in return for improved pensions and other state income maintenance measures. The 1975 Act served to raise the stakes in the debate on pensions in the country as a whole, and can be said to have led eventually to a breakdown in the bipartisan approach of the two main political parties. However, in the short term the prospects for pensioners improved dramatically.

The Conservative Radicalism of the 1980s

> There was a transformation in the political conduct of institutional change in this country. During the earlier part of my lifetime, during the fifties, sixties and seventies, there were a lot of disagreements between left and right, but on the whole, both sets of governments supported the continuation of the welfare state. They [the Conservatives] may not have wished to make such generous benefit improvements as the Labour side, but they were very much committed to the postwar establishment of the welfare state. (Prof. Peter Townsend, leading academic and activist, OPPOL interview)

Fundamental to the welfare state consensus was the contributory retirement pension. The state was responsible for administrating a scheme which ensured that those who paid National Insurance contributions would receive a pension that reflected their contribution. With the election of Mrs Thatcher and the Conservative Party in 1979, the contributory principle, and the entire concept of National Insurance, was no longer taken for granted. The Tories, led by Margaret Thatcher, were in no mood to compromise when they gained power in 1979. The Conservative election victory signalled the end of what remained of a bipartisan approach to pensions policy. SERPS was immediately revised, having come into operation only in April 1978,[26] and the annual rise to the basic pension was

Chart 7.1 Loss of value to the pension from decoupling the link with earnings 1978-1999

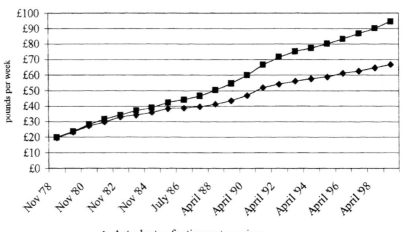

—◆— Actual rate of retirement pensions

—■— Rate based on increase of higher of prices or earnings

Source: Authors' analysis of data given in a Parliamentary answer, 1999.

pegged to the Retail Price Index. The Conservatives removed the link with national average earnings and thus in the long term decoupled the value of the pension from the general rise in living standards in the country. It was a dramatic change of policy and would have far-reaching consequences for pensioners and the movement (Townsend, 1999). The long-term consequence was to erode the value of the state pension, obliging many older people to claim means-tested benefits. Thus it was an essential first step in 'rolling back the state' in terms of its role in the provision of income in old age and substituting market-based mechanisms. This policy has steadily eroded the relative value of the state pension (see Chart 7.1). As Ginn and Arber reported (1999:156), quoting Johnson (1994) and Hills

---

[26] Employers and employees were encouraged to contract out of the scheme and to take out money purchase schemes instead. By extending the arrangements for contracting out of SERPS, the real value of the scheme – its generality – was compromised.

(1993): 'as a result by 1994 a third of pensioners required means-tested benefits, while those with small additional pensions (less than £40 a week in 1993) faced a poverty trap, receiving little financial benefit from them'.

These changes were a dramatic change of policy, and dealt a serious blow to the pensioners' movement, and to the leadership in particular:

> They had established this National Pensioners' Convention, which on the face of it had brought most of the powerful interests together in an alliance and suddenly it was just completely not being recognised. (An informed London advocate for older people, OPPOL interview)

The pensioners' movement had to adapt to a situation in which it no longer had systematic access to ministers, its major allies suffered a significant loss of influence, and previous bipartisan approaches to pensions ceased. The partial decommissioning of SERPS was the first case in the UK of a government imposing a reduction in the returns on a pension scheme without cross-party support.

There was little initial reaction from the pensioners' movement to the abolition of the link between pensions and earnings, one of the reasons being that its consequences were not obvious at the time. The link with prices was maintained and the predominant fear was of the consequences of price inflation as a legacy of the 1970s. Further, economic recession restricted wage improvements for working people and in some cases reduced them significantly. Thus the cumulative effect of small annual percentage differences between incomes and prices had not started to bite.

In the early 1980s there were few signs that the Conservatives were going to remain in power for nearly two decades. Further, it was still not clear that the Conservatives' policies were aimed at abolishing a major part of the welfare state, as this had not been their stance in the past. The 1986 Social Security Act, which claimed to 'reform' Social Security, set in motion trends that would further undermine the foundations of the state pension. It reduced the SERPS benefits to 20% of average revalued earnings instead of 25%, to be calculated over a working life of forty-four years for women and forty-nine for men instead of the best twenty years. The rationale for the move was to limit the future financial liabilities of the Exchequer.

These legislative changes allowed employers to contract out of the state earnings-related scheme, and offered both employers and employees incentives to take out money purchase schemes instead. In addition, the Conservatives took substantial steps to place privately bought pension schemes at an advantage. With hindsight some of incentives might be thought to have misfired in the long term. These incentives played a part in bringing private pensions into disrepute through the scandal over mis-selling of pensions that subsequently emerged. In the early 1990s it became clear that some companies had inappropriately sold private pensions that left their customers less well off than they would have been had they stayed with their original schemes.

In the end the Conservative governments between 1979 and 1997 did not abolish SERPS. This may be seen as a positive sign of the influence of the pensioners' movement. However, the range of benefits in the scheme and eligibility criteria were changed significantly to reduce its long-term cost to government and to reduce its value to eventual recipients. The Conservative victory at the polls in 1992, albeit with a much reduced majority, saw the party maintain its tough stance on pensions. In 1995 they further reduced the ratio of benefits to contributions in state-run schemes by phasing in an increase in the age of pension entitlement from 60 to 65 for women.

New Labour and Pensions

Through the 1990s there was a revival of pensioner activity in general and the National Pensioners' Convention in particular. Systematic opposition to what was happening to the state pension became the focus of attention and interested parties sought to coordinate their activities. The pensioner organisations took an active role in trying to shape the policy of the potential Labour administration. The Labour Party, having made commitments to raise the basic pension in its 1992 manifesto, then became increasingly noncommittal on the subject:

> ...in opposition we met with Blair and Gordon Brown and people like that, Harriet Harman. Always they were saying, yes, the basic pension will be the bedrock or foundation. They never absolutely committed themselves to restoring the link; it was mainly the issue of raising the pension to a reasonable amount. You see, the government's idea was not to have an absolute commitment but to go into it with us and the impression given was that it would be a jointly investigated thing, and we took that on face value. (Jack Jones, NPC President, OPPOL interview)

In June 1996 the Labour Party published a policy document called 'Security in Retirement'. It specifically refrained from committing the party to restoring the link with earnings, questioning the feasibility of undoing the damage done by the Tories to SERPS, and putting the idea of private pension schemes firmly on the New Labour agenda. At the Labour Party Conference the same year, Barbara Castle made an impassioned speech on the need to 'restore the link', but Jack Jones, the mainstay of the organised pensioners' movement, chose to accept the promise of a fundamental review of pensions in the place of a firm commitment to restore the link in the Party's forthcoming manifesto. It was a decision he would come to regret.

Whereas in 1992 the Labour manifesto had offered precise figures of rises in pensions as part of a package of measures designed to combat poverty among the elderly and young families, the 1997 manifesto simply promised to raise the basic pension 'in line with prices' and included a commitment to ensuring that pensioners would share in 'the increasing prosperity of the nation'. The precise meaning of this commitment and how it was to be achieved was not elaborated. Tony Blair had, however, succeeded in reducing the issue to a sideshow. While Blair proclaimed in his speech to the Labour Party conference in September 1997 that Britain could be, under his leadership, 'the best place to live, the best place to bring up children, the best place to lead a fulfilled life, the best place to grow old', the Labour Party had entered into the 1997 General Election with a commitment to follow the Conservative government's financial guidelines for the first two years of their administration. Pension commitments were not to interfere with a reputation for financial prudence.

Green Paper Proposals

Expectations of the New Labour government were high among the various pensioners' organisations. This was understandable, given the fact that the bulk of the membership of the NPC was affiliated through retired members' sections of trade unions. These people were acutely conscious of the difficulties faced by the Parliamentary Labour Party over the years and understood the need to maintain unity within the party in the run-up to an election. These same people would be less forgiving of the newly elected Labour government once it became clear that New Labour's pensions policy was in essence a continuation of the approach of the previous administration. In practice, New Labour have maintained the policy of a link with prices but not with earnings, and this has led to a sense amongst pensioner activists of being let down.

On 17 July 1997, the Social Security Secretary, Harriet Harman, officially launched the pensions review promised in Labour's election manifesto, promising a 'special role' to Jack Jones and the NPC (DSS press release, 17 July 1997). In September 1997 she announced a timetable for action and said 'the review was already making swift progress'. Eventually, after repeated delays, the government's Green Paper (cm 4179) on pensions, 'A New Contract for Welfare: Partnership in Pensions', was issued on 15 December 1998. The dilemma for the New Labour government is reflected in the contrasting rhetoric contained in the document. The Green Paper was introduced by Tony Blair using the language of 'insurance and contract'. He declared that:

> These reforms mean that the total income of pensioners will rise in years to come, mainly fuelled by rising private contributions. Public spending on pensions will rise too in real terms, but less sharply, and will fall as a proportion of national income. This will ensure that the pension system remains both fair and affordable. This is our New Insurance Contract for pensions. This Contract will deliver the security we all want, now and for the future. (Department of Social Security, 1998: foreword)

However, the thrust of the paper itself is about targeting the poorest through the use of means testing and the Minimum Income Guarantee (MIG). The two other major proposals in the Green Paper were improved pensions for carers and others with no or little contribution record (a suggestion that was widely welcomed) and 'stakeholder' pensions to encourage savings for private pensions lower down the income scale. The Treasury language of affordability is strongly present and the long-term financial objectives for public expenditure are made clear.

> Public spending on pensions will decline as a share of GDP, from 5.4 per cent today to 4.5 per cent in 2050. By 2050, the proportion of pensioner incomes coming from the State, now 60 per cent, will have fallen to 40 per cent, and the proportion coming from private pension provision will have increased from 40 to 60 per cent. This will ensure that the pension system remains both fair and affordable. (Department of Social Security, 1998: paragraph 41)

The pensioners' movement found nothing in the Green Paper to suggest that the submissions made by the NPC had been taken seriously. Their conclusion was that there had never been any intention on the part of the Labour leadership to alter its plans on pensions as laid out in the 1996 policy document. In effect the deterioration of the relationship between New Labour and the pensioners' movement hinges on the way the pensions review not only did not take up any of the recommendations made by representatives of the movement, but also proceeded to lay the groundwork for a policy that would promote means testing of pensioners. It came as no surprise, therefore, that in the aftermath of the review it was the low take-up rate of means-tested benefits that most exercised government ministers, including the minister for pensions.[27]

---

[27] The budget statement in March 1998 estimated that six to seven hundred thousand people did not claim the Minimum Income Guarantee to which they were entitled and announced that the DSS would be setting up nine pilot projects to identify the best way to

The 1946 National Insurance Act had recognised that the provision made by the Poor Law was inadequate,[28] and that the general feeling was that claiming means-tested help from the Assistance Board was a humiliating experience. The insurance principle was felt to bestow rights rather than charity. In April 1999 the government introduced the MIG, allowing £75 per week for single pensioners and £116.60 per week for pensioner couples. However, while this provided a safety net for those who claimed it, it also signalled a tough stance on the vexed question of raising the state pension itself. No new money was added to the state pension beyond the established price inflation index, which had fallen to a thirty-year low. The MIG was, in practice, a collection of means-tested benefits and thus denied to anyone who had savings of over £8,000. It became clear that there was an intention to make this means-tested benefit the mainstay of income support in old age. The government, in accepting that the state pension was below the Minimum Income Guarantee, also accepted that a high proportion of all older people would be claiming Income Support in the future.

Under the terms of the government's reforms, the diminishing value of the state pension would mean that increasing numbers of pensioners would rely on means-tested benefits to achieve a minimum standard of living. Despite the government's insistence that its intention was to target those most in need, it had effectively devised a system that suggested a return to the means-testing system which the pensioners' movement had traditionally opposed. Ultimately, it was not the amount of the basic pension so much as the return to the pre-1940 situation that lay at the heart of the pensioners' movement's refusal to concede the argument for 'targeting'.

The MIG was seen by the pensioners' movement as paving the way to means-testing the basic pension. No matter how often the government insists that the intention is to target the poorest pensioners, in order to see that the money is spent only on those in genuine need, the pensioners' movement sees such a policy as a deliberate ploy to avoid the national responsibility to provide an adequate pension, and as a betrayal of the principle of universal provision (a principle seen as central to the creation of the welfare state itself).

---

get pensioners to claim benefits to which they were entitled.
[28] Established in Elizabethan times, the Poor Law survived, in terms of the principles it embodied, for over three centuries until the welfare state arrived in force with the 1934 Unemployment Assistance Act.

SERPS and the Stakeholder Pension – The Shape of New Labour's Policy Becomes Clear

It was not only pensioners themselves who insisted on the validity of the contributory principle, which means that the value of your pension is based on contributions made rather than on an assessment of your current income. Frank Field, formerly the minister charged with pension reform, submitted a damning memorandum to the Committee on Social Security (November 1999) supporting that principle:

> This government's original Green Paper on welfare reform, New Ambitions for our Country: A New Contract for Welfare, was published in March 1998. As the title suggests this Green Paper promised to centre welfare reforms around the principle of the contract. This approach was adopted for many of the good reasons that can be adduced in favour of the contributory principle. Strong support for the principles underpinning this document was a 'key finding' of the Department of Social Security's Attitudes to the Welfare State and the Response to Reform. The entire cabinet approved the text of the Green Paper too, part of which read: 'The development of the contract will lead to greater trust—with a clearer contract, people can have greater confidence that they will get proper protection in return for the contributions they make.' (Cm 3805, paragraph 11.6)

The ministerial team led by Alistair Darling, which replaced that led by Harriet Harman (including Frank Field), introduced a welfare reform package containing significant changes to the pensions system, including the stakeholder pension. Perhaps the most radical change in the entire package of reforms was the decision to abolish SERPS and replace it with a means-tested State Second Pension (SSP).[29] The decision to abolish the scheme was ostensibly about flexibility in a fluid job market but was probably also motivated by the fact that it would save the state from a significant future financial commitment.[30] SERPS was a widely respected scheme, setting the standard for occupational pensions, and had come to be seen by the pensioners' movement, despite some initial reservations, as 'a

---

[29] The SSP will be paid at a flat rate to those earning below about £9,000 a year. Those earning more will be expected to provide for themselves, albeit with generous rebates. SERPS was explicitly designed to appeal to the better off, by ensuring that those who earn more get more on retirement. The SSP, worth proportionately much more to the very poorest, inverts this principle.

[30] There was debate about the actual future cost of SERPS. The changes introduced by the Conservatives had dramatically reduced the long-term costs. The ABI calculated that 'if the generosity of SERPS had not been reduced, nor the state pension age equalised, then the cost to the state would be closer to £87 billion in 2040', as opposed to around £20 billion (Stears, 1998:11). The affordability of the scheme was essentially a matter of political priorities.

commendable, and, more importantly, workable scheme which should have been preserved' (Tony Lynes, Pensions Policy Advisor, speaking at the NPC 6th Annual School, 20-22 October 1999, The Wedgwood Memorial College, Barlaston Village, Stoke-on-Trent).

Initially neither the pensions industry nor the pensioners' movement showed much enthusiasm for the stakeholder pension. The NPC identified flaws in the government's stakeholder schemes, which it concluded 'will generally be money purchase schemes providing pensions of unpredictable value and involving substantial risks for their members' (Lynes, 2000:5). In political terms, these changes found a small audience among older people, as they addressed future pensioners and had no impact on the condition of current pensioners. There has been an underwhelming public response to the changes. Most of the public are either unaware of them or regard pensions as too complicated to understand. The extension of individual private pensions has also been met with consumer resistance (Williams et al.,1999). The large number of victims of the pensions mis-selling scandal, which occurred when the Conservative government sought to promote individual private pensions in the mid-1990s, provides an impediment to the popularity of schemes that are perceived as being run for a profit.[31]

The problem for the New Labour ministers who tried to persuade the pensioners belonging to the movement of the pragmatic nature of the government's position is that they find their audience reverting to the clarion call of restoring the link with earnings:

> People by and large have rather surprisingly recognised that, ok, that it is a sensible approach given that resources are scarce ... but the trouble is that (maybe it is the influence of the NPC or what Jack Jones has done) despite people rationally recognising the sense of the strategy that I've described, people do actually quickly move back to the 'then why not restore the earnings?' thing. (Stephen Timms, Minister for Social Security and Chairman of the Inter-Ministerial Group, 1999, OPPOL interview)

The post of minister responsible for pensions changed hands four times in the first two years of the Labour government. Reshuffling ministers is nothing unusual, but the lack of a consistent voice in so complex an area of policy did suggest that the post was one that ministers found uncomfortable, especially given the otherwise stable nature of the

---

[31] The problem came to public notice in December 1993 with the publication of a report on the standards of pension transfer sales, in which some 83% of sampled files were classed as unsatisfactory according to the standards set by the Financial Services Act. The insurance companies involved have shown themselves extremely reluctant to take responsibility and to settle claims for mis-selling, provoking a government 'name and shame' campaign in 1997.

Blair cabinet compared to that of many of its predecessors. With the appointment of Jeff Rooker as Minister for Social Security with special responsibility for pensions in July 1999, the government made it plain that the conciliatory stance of his predecessors, all three of them, was a thing of the past. Invited to attend a fringe meeting at the Labour Party conference in October 1999, Jeff Rooker stood his ground against Jack Jones, Barbara Castle, Tony Benn and a hostile audience of pensioners. The clash on the same issue on the floor of the 2000 conference would see the platform defeated, an almost unique occurrence under Blair's leadership. Nevertheless the Labour leadership would declare itself willing to ignore their defeat.

Later in 1999, addressing a conference organised by the National Association of Pension Funds (NAPF), Jeff Rooker, stated categorically that the pension, introduced as part of the welfare state, had 'never provided a decent standard of living'. His speech warned workers that they faced 'abject poverty' if they relied on the basic state pension (*Financial Times*, 21 October 1999). This was to be the clearest statement from a Labour minister about the sliding value of the state pension, echoing Michael Portillo's controversial claim, as Conservative Chief Secretary to the Treasury several years earlier, that the pension would be 'worth a nugatory amount in the coming century'.

In March 1999 the government had announced a '£1 billion pensioner package' consisting of a £100 Winter Fuel Payment (the existing payment was £20), and an uprating of the MIG in line with earnings.[32] Pensioners were, according to government figures, considerably better off as a result. The Minimum Tax Guarantee apparently meant that two-thirds of pensioners would not pay any income tax, implicitly acknowledging that the majority of pensioners were living on an annual income of less than £6,000. However, the biggest single factor in formulating public opinion on the Labour record on pensions was the announcement of an inflation-only increase to the state pension of 75p, made while Labour were also proclaiming the way that their economic policies had brought prosperity to the nation.

In the face of adverse publicity and public reaction, Labour sought to stem the criticism, first with publicity, then with some real resources, but ultimately without altering the long-term Treasury policy of minimising

---

[32] There is no guarantee that the MIG will remain linked to earnings, as it appears that this would be a disincentive to people who are, as low earners, the target population for the stakeholder pension: 'While MIG is tied to earnings it is likely to make a stakeholder poor value, or even valueless, to many of the target population' (Association of British Insurers briefing paper, Stakeholder Pensions: Drawing Together the Threads, 1999:3).

direct state involvement in pension provision.[33] In early 2000 Labour stepped up their efforts to persuade people of their determination to address pensioner poverty. A Pensioners' Campaign Pack was sent to party activists in anticipation of local elections. The pack included a 'direct mail letter for Labour and weak Labour voters' in which people were asked to assist in identifying pensioners who were not claiming the MIG. The package provided proof of New Labour's concern for older people, and to some extent allayed misgivings among Labour activists. However, as far as activists within the pensioners' movement were concerned, the government, in refusing to raise the basic pension to the level of the Minimum Income Guarantee, was failing in its duty to pay to all pensioners an adequate basic pension, which at the very least would be equivalent to the MIG. In refusing to accede to the demand for a basic pension of £75, a demand made in a petition signed by 100,000 people and delivered to 10 Downing Street by Jack Jones and others on 28 July 1999,[34] the government demonstrated its determination not to give ground to the pensioners.

Labour's current message is clearly that the role of the government is to focus on those in the greatest need. When questioned about raising the basic state pension in line with earnings to give every pensioner a right to a certain standard of living, Jeff Rooker replies simply, 'Every election we fought with that issue we lost'.

> The basic state pension is what it says it is, the *basic* state pension. It is not pensioner income – I will not accept and join in the debate talking about the basic state pension as though it was pensioners' total income. It isn't; it forms half of the average pensioner's income. Pensioners' incomes are keeping apace, as opposed to the basic state pension ... people retire today either with SERPS or with occupational pension schemes; the average couple has £240 quid and the single person £129 net, that's *net*. So the idea that the vast majority of people are living on the basic state pension is bullshit; they are not, and people that perpetuate that myth can't have a proper debate because you are debating different things – our job in government, as a Labour government, is to get the money to those who need it most, and those who need it most are not getting £129 a week, they are only getting £66.75 because they weren't allowed to have a second pension, they weren't in an occupational pension, they were low paid or they got the basic pension, and they've no savings ... and we've made a

---

[33] Macnicol (2000) describes in the detail the Treasury resistance to reform of pensions leading up to the enactment of the 1942 Beveridge report, including overtly political intervention by Senior Civil Servants. The parallels between current debates and those of the pre-war era in terms of arguments and protagonists are striking.

[34] The petition was supported by Age Concern and Help the Aged.

provision to get them an extra ten quid a week, from the MIG, means-tested, I accept that, but that's where we've targeted our resources, and we make no apologies about that. (Jeff Rooker, Labour minister for pensions, OPPOL interview)

Thus the main lesson of the recent history of the politics over pensions is that all parties in power for the last twenty years have sought to reduce the role of the state in the provision of pensions and have not responded to the pensioners' movement's foremost demand for a state pension linked to earnings. Electorally the significant issue has been not state responsibility, but taxation. The political parties have to reconcile the public's expectations of state provision with its willingness to pay taxation. Taxation has always been a major election issue. Labour strategists suggest that the party lost the 1992 election because they gave priority to welfare rather than taxation policies. Placing too much importance on welfare issues labelled a party as a 'tax and spend' party. New Labour attitudes are firmly embedded in a belief that the 1997 election was won with the promise of no taxation rises. On the other hand, the systematic devaluation of the basic pension, and its decline in relation to other sources of pensioner income, has undermined some of the solidarity and commitment of the electorate to the institution. Although the specific campaign for £75 in '99 raised 100,000 signatures this was not particularly successful, certainly when compared to pensioners' petitions in the past, for example the two-million-strong petition presented to Parliament in 1940. The '£75 in '99' campaign achieved no significant response from government at the time. However, the electoral apathy from Labour's core support in the local and European elections in 2000 stimulated Gordon Brown, the Chancellor of the Exchequer, to direct significant funds towards pensioners to try to redeem Labour's image as a 'caring' party.

To understand the present situation of the pensioners' movement, it is necessary to review the situation in 1998, when the realities of New Labour's pensions policy, and of the failure of the movement to influence that policy, first became clear to the movement's rank and file. This is seen by some activists as a turning point for pensioners' organisations. It would appear that the disillusion of the movement at that time, both with New Labour and with the movement's leadership, was a reaction to what was seen by many as the inability of Jack Jones to carry weight with the government. At this point there was the potential for the pensioners' movement to split into more or less radical factions. Jack Jones's 1996 acceptance of a promise from the Labour Party to review pensions rather than a manifesto pledge to restore the link between pensions and earnings has been the subject of criticism by some. This failure was seen by some influential members of the BPTUAA as a watershed in the history of the movement. In the aftermath of that Labour conference, feelings among the rank and file of the movement ran high. The *British Pensioner* in particular took a very critical view of the NPC's leadership, running the headline 'Was it betrayal?' It is not the purpose of this chapter to analyse the complex relationship between the NPC and the BPTUAA. However, in distancing itself from Jack Jones, the BPTUAA confirmed its ability to act independently of the NPC. It also allowed discussion of a new strategy, one that would express the resentment felt by the activists of the movement, many of whom had long desired a more radical approach to the campaign.

In May 1999 delegates at the Pensioners' Parliament held at Blackpool were united in their condemnation of the government's policy on pensions. Recognising their inability to influence government by traditional means, they turned their attention to the question of direct action. The Pensioners' Rights Campaign (PRC) stepped up its actions in the North and the Midlands,[35] drawing on support from those regions that have traditionally felt excluded from the National Pensioners' Convention, which has its headquarters in London. Holding a rally in Manchester Town Hall on 15 June 1999, the PRC was delighted by a speech made by the one guest speaker who had managed to make the journey north, Bruce Kent, who stated that:

> we have to all relearn our history, because we are not making much progress – the government listens to us, we go along and have a chat, we have some tea and sandwiches, and at the end of the day nothing happens, absolutely nothing happens – they love long discussions, be they Conservative or be they Labour; it fobs people off, it takes the heat out of discussions....

Jack Jones was by no means persuaded of the value of direct action, and the '£75 in '99' campaign can be seen as an attempt to regain the initiative. There was amongst sections of the pensioners' movement an increasing dissatisfaction with traditional alliances and strategies. Some felt the unions were failing to act in support of the campaign for the restoration of the earnings link, and such views were voiced, for example, at the Camden Conference, which the NPC organised in January 1999 in response to the Green Paper. Attended by 150 representatives of pensioners'

---

[35] This organisation proclaims itself 'a radical organisation for retired citizens, composed of autonomous regional councils, with affiliated branches of senior citizens' (Pensioners' Charter leaflet, October 1998). The Pensioners' Rights Campaign, in July 1990, staged what is apparently the first attempt at direct action by the pensioners' movement when it attempted to block traffic on Westminster Bridge.

organisations and other interested groups, the conference focused on the inadequacy of the Green Paper proposals and the need to establish links with other disaffected groups. In effect, the conference, which signalled the end of the movement's cooperation with government, also demonstrated impatience with the traditional forms of protest, and the behind-the-scenes style of lobbying favoured by Jack Jones. These debates took place within the overriding need to sustain a credible unified campaign,[36] and, for example, efforts were made in December 1999 to organise a southwest region, with a conference in Taunton, bringing together delegates from pensioners' groups from Cornwall, Devon, Somerset, Dorset, Wiltshire, Hampshire, Gloucestershire and Bristol. The growing sense of disillusionment felt by pensioner activists had to be channelled, but in which direction?

Conclusion

The pensioners' movement's dashed expectations of the Green Paper were arrived at through an intensely political process. There was a mechanism for an open process of consultation, but there was the realpolitik – a balance of political pressures inside and outside Whitehall. In this complex process of policy formation, some social forces proved more influential than others. The pensions industry was able to make its voice heard effectively at ministerial level, for example the Association of British Insurers have felt able to support the basic thrust of New Labour policy. Perhaps even more decisive has been the attitudes of the Treasury establishment and its orientation to the world of international finance. Their concerns certainly appear to have weighed very heavily, enforcing what they see as prudent financial discipline. The pensioners' movement, on the other hand, although able to offer expert advice[37] and to articulate the voice of pensioners themselves, had to suffer the humiliation of seeing its experts snubbed and its advice ignored.

Generally speaking, pensions policy has been perceived as distinct from the political process in Britain – 'a mandarin affair best left to actuaries and civil servants' (Miles, 1994:6). In the real world, the extent to which the state pension system is enlarged and the area of its operation are determined almost entirely by political and economic judgements of

---

[36] The case for a unified movement was eloquently made by Professor Alan Walker, the Patron of the NPC, in a 1992 speech in which he said that 'the living standards and basic human dignity of millions of pensioners depend on it. Your movement has vital work to do and, if you are to achieve your goal, you must be united'.

[37] See *Pensions – Who Pays?*, published by the NPC in 1999, in which the argument for indexing the basic pension to average wages is discussed.

established elites (Pilch and Wood, 1979:155). The immediate problem for the pensioners' movement is how to combat the strait-jacket of financial imperatives as perceived by successive governments. Pensioners' organisations have great difficulty in influencing governments that base their attitude to pensions and welfare on a belief that the state should limit its role. Governments feel that globalisation and in particular international financial pressures over taxation and state expenditure preclude them from making long-term financial guarantees on pensions (Mishra, 1999).

It is not by chance that the earnings link is not restored – nor will it ever be restored by governments of either major party in the foreseeable future – because the principles of universal payments and social insurance have been removed from the dominant agenda of policy on pensions. Given the government's reluctance to articulate the long-term future of the basic state pension, one needs to look outside government policy explanations to fully appreciate the situation. The European Commission, for example, provides clear documentary evidence of the situation.

> The yearly gap between earnings and basic pension dynamics will reduce the ratio of the latter to average male earnings from 15% in 1995 to 10% in 2020 and 7% in 2050. (*European Economy*, No. 3:103)

Phasing out the basic pension is the means by which governments shed large potential future financial liabilities. This looks good to international financiers looking to place 'footloose' capital and avoids the politically risky business of raising contribution rates. If pensions were linked to earnings, the required rates of contribution would have to rise. This looks too much like raising taxes at a time of political competition between Labour and the Conservatives over cutting taxes. If the basic pension continues to lose its value, it will eventually become no more than an anomalous vestige of an outdated system, and as such will be entirely subsumed within a means-tested benefits system. While it is not feasible politically to abolish the state pension (see Chapter 8 on the power of 'compassionate ageism'), in practice it will be abolished by default.

The loss of power by the nation-state in the face of an international competitive market provides a context for understanding the problems of the Blair government. The New Labour government proclaimed itself ready for major welfare reform but has so far failed to deliver. They are not short of money, given the reported burgeoning tax returns, yet they have not produced the radical and coherent reform of welfare they promised – the details of which were always somewhat vague whilst in opposition. Indeed, all the key ministers have been replaced and there is still a lack of a clear long-term strategy for a way forward for welfare reform. The only resignations from the Blair administration over policy differences have come over welfare issues: Harriet Harman and Frank Field lost their positions over these problems. The allocation of increased resources for older people through the winter heating allowance and free television licence is a clear symptom of a lack of direction. These increased allowances produce no long-term commitments for the Treasury, nor do they presage a resolution to the key issues of the future relationship of the state to health, welfare and pension provision. An important component of the programme also appears to be to lower people's expectations of the state, and thus persuade the next generation to use individual savings to prepare for old age.

It is possible to see themes that have developed over the existence of the New Labour regime. These are signposted most clearly in the actions that have been taken rather than the rhetoric in which policies have been expressed. There appears to be a desire to limit and contain the long-term financial obligations of the state, and to facilitate the participation of private capital and encourage private provision to substitute for public wherever possible. The Blairite 'Third Way' seems to accept that there are severe limits on what the welfare state can provide in the future (whether this is due to demography or an unwillingness to raise taxation is unclear). The consequence is to seek to limit welfare to a minority, as a safety net for a small group at the bottom of society, and to encourage self/private provision for the majority. The thrust of pension reform seems unclear, but the prime initiative, the stakeholder pension, is to extend individual saving for old age further down the social scale. On pension reform the thrust has been to bring the benefits of work-based earnings-related schemes within the reach of a broader section of the population. What is not discernible is action on the erosion of basic state pension entitlement. The guaranteed minimum income for pensioners is in fact a complex means-tested safety net. In the long term it is inevitable that the incompatibility between attracting the low-paid into stakeholder pensions and a means-tested MIG, which will take away much of the benefit from such pensions, will become a source of tension.

'Affordability' is one rhetorical linchpin of the debate. It is a firmly held belief among pensioners belonging to the movement that the Welfare State is affordable. But fears that the state pension will not survive for lack of funding are widespread; Hawkes and Garman (1995) found that fewer than one in ten of those aged under 35 are 'very confident' that they will receive a state pension when they retire. Although there have been government promises to maintain the state pension, there is a widespread belief, fuelled by apocalyptic demography, that an ageing population will inevitably require the state pension to be withdrawn (Mullan, 2000). Blackburn (1999:4) observes:

> State pensions are threatened everywhere, as the tax-raising powers of government are squeezed, and as the greying of the population requires today's workforce to support ever-larger numbers of the retired. The latter, having themselves paid a lifetime of contributions and taxes geared to more generous provision, find that their income plummets on retirement – in the UK the basic pension is less than a fifth of average earnings.

The pensioners' movement shows every indication of holding to its basic position, which is that the state pension can be afforded, and the government, were it genuinely interested in supporting the Welfare State, would strengthen the National Insurance scheme. The basic state pension, as a payment made to older people only, remains the one payment that offers older people a unique status within the system. Its continuation is undermined by a welfare system that increasingly relies on means-testing as a means of identifying eligibility for benefits. The case for spending money on those people who are most in need seems difficult to refute, but the pensioners' movement remains committed to the view that the right way to do this for older people is through the traditional principle of universal payment.

8 Older People and Public Opinion

Introduction

Like the rest of the population, older people vary in terms of their economic positions, political views, interests, capacities and activities. However, the social process, by its nature, requires us to categorise groups of people. These social categories can harden into stereotypes. Further, as Binstock and Day (1995:12), citing Estes (1997, 1992) emphasise, these socially constructed images and definitions can prove more important to the individual experiences and problems of old age than the objective facts and conditions of the elderly.

The media, the government and organisations working on behalf of older people publicise and legitimise different definitions of old age. These definitions identify particular characteristics as typical and important with respect to older people. These stereotypes and how they are presented can contribute to 'the socially constructed images of the elderly as a problem and help implement policies based on often misleading stereotypes' (Pampel, 1998:12-13). The first part of this chapter sets out the nature and origins of two contrasting stereotypes of older people and examines their implications for old-age politics. The second part examines empirical evidence gathered by our project as to the prevalence and impact of these stereotypes.

Contrasting Stereotypes of the Older Population

Scapegoat Ageism

A shift in opinion is occurring. Increasing media hype about our ageing population and an increase in independently funded retirements could be the cause of an emerging new stereotype of older people. This new stereotype views the aged not only as affluent and advantaged in relation to younger age groups, but, at the extreme, as selfish and greedy and dominating the state economy. Binstock (1994) refers to this perspective as 'scapegoat ageism'. The increase in numbers of dependent elderly members of society is juxtaposed to a decrease in numbers of working-age people.

There is a fear that the decreasing working population will not be able to support the increasing retired population. While younger people have to work to pay social security benefits for an ever-increasing population of older people, the older people themselves, scapegoat ageism would have us believe, are living it up, travelling and playing golf.

Scapegoat ageism has a number of facets. The major components of the stereotype are an affluent lifestyle, hedonism and an unfair taking advantage of the welfare system. The hedonism and affluent lifestyle aspects of the image may be illustrated by car stickers that proclaim 'recycled teenager – spending the kids inheritance' and by modern idioms such as 'greedy geezers' or 'permaholiday' (referring to long holidays taken by affluent pensioners) reported by those monitoring language change. An article in The *Independent* described over-50s as going on adventure holidays and regularly eating out. It advises advertisers that 'the over-50s market is highly lucrative' (Carter, 1999). A *Times* article, although describing the newly retired as the richest group of people in Britain, clearly acknowledged this is not the case for all pensioners. There is still a sense that over-70s live modestly and struggle to make ends meet. 'Once they hit 70, however, their wealth starts to run down, partly out of necessity and partly out of a growing belief that it makes more sense to spend their savings on themselves before they die than to leave substantial bequests' (Frean, 1999:6). Although the existence of a minority of very poor elderly is not to be denied, there is an apparent growing perception, reflected in the media, that poor pensioners will soon be a thing of the past as the next generation of affluent older consumers, now in early retirement, takes their place.

This quote from an American website illustrates how the moral status of the different generations is reconstructed under scapegoat ageism.

> I'm willing to risk being placed in the doghouse by some older folks and their well-heeled, well-oiled lobbyists for saying these things, because I'm bothered by constantly hearing what a bunch of reckless spenders my generation is. Sure, most of us whippersnappers don't save enough. Maybe somebody ought to start asking why. It's because we're taxed to the hilt to pay for our parents' Social Security and Medicare programs. (Fulks, 1996)

This stereotype links directly with the 'timebomb' image of ageing discussed in Chapter 2.

Compassionate Ageism

Until recently, older people have frequently been stereotyped as vulnerable and deserving. One view of the elderly defines them as both impoverished and financially dependent, and frail and physically dependent. As a result they are sometimes seen as a burden to their families and the working population in general. On the whole, however, older people who have preserved their moral reputation are seen as deserving of physical care and financial support. Pampel (1998) has termed this kind of stereotyping 'compassionate ageism'.

Although this is changing to some extent, older people have in the past been amongst the poorest sections of the population (Walker, 1992; Walker and Walker, 1997; Vincent, 1995; Arber and Ginn, 1991). There is a long historical tradition of the elderly poor being supported by charity – it is still possible to find almshouses in most British communities. Older people as a group are seen as dependent not only because of their disadvantaged material condition (Phillipson and Walker, 1986; Walker, 1992a) but also through physical frailty (Mulley, 1997). The 'old' are seen as characterised by loss: loss of senses (sight and hearing), loss of mobility, and loss of mind. Thus the debate about older people enters the public arena under the heading of *Welfare*. Older peoples' welfare requirements are very visible in the political arena and such images are continually legitimised though the portrayal of helpless older people by the media (Carrigan and Szmigin, 2000). This compassionate ageism is also illustrated by the images of older people portrayed in party political manifestos.

Images of Older People in Party Political Manifestos

The history of British social welfare since the Elizabethan era has been a series of attempts to differentiate the 'deserving poor' who should receive the support of the community from the feckless individuals who are in need only as a result of their own shortcomings. The rhetoric of the 'deserving poor' is central to the images of older people used by the political parties in contemporary Britain. This rhetoric is general to all parties – the manifestos conjure pictures of hard-working citizens in reduced circumstances who deserve their share of the national wealth. Work is seen as particularly meritorious and an essential part of the necessary characteristic of those in receipt of state funds (cf. Bauman, 1998). For example, in 1950, the case of working pensioners was taken up in the manifestos of both the Conservatives and the Liberals, both of whom were in opposition at the time. They both proposed abolishing the means test on working pensioners.

> Old Age pensioners who wish to go on working are performing a great public service, and a Liberal Government would revoke the Means Test on the working pensioner. (Liberal Manifesto 1950)

We can examine the two components of the stereotype, 'the deserving' and 'the poor'. Some special categories – widows, war pensioners, ex-servicemen in general – are seen as particularly deserving. Behaviours seen as particularly deserving are good citizenship and service. The idea that those who have contributed to the nation throughout their lives deserve consideration in old age has been used to justify the pension in general, as well as particular kinds of additional pension.

> We have lowered the age at which increases in public service and armed forces pensions become payable, and we have further improved the position of war pensioners and their widows. Public service pensions, armed forces pensions and supplementary pensions are all now reviewed every single year, together with the main national insurance benefits. (Conservative Manifesto, February, 1974)

The manifestos identify their opponents as either cheating these worthy people of their just rewards or of preventing them from realising the benefits of their own efforts. Older people in general, however, tend not to be differentiated in the manifestos. They are collectively presented as part of 'the poor'. The case for food subsidies in the 1950s, for example, was made by an appeal for compassion for the old as a poor and deserving section of the population.

The manifestos can be deconstructed to reveal an implicit class analysis. Parties identify the key interests of older people and pensioners in specific ways that tend to be indicative of their more general approach to society. For example, Labour's 1997 view of social extremes in Britain is expressed in their manifesto: 'We are a national party, supported today by people from all walks of life, from the successful businessman or woman to the pensioner on a council estate.' This statement carries within it an explicit denial of representing a class, along with an implicit acknowledgement of class difference and an assumption that old age and poverty go together. Over the postwar period, for Labour, pensioners have been part of the mass of poor; they are part of an unequal society. For Conservatives and Liberals the issue of poverty in old age is, in contrast, a problem about fixed incomes, savings and the value of money and capital. The Liberal Party (and its successors) like to present themselves as outside the class struggle of employers against workers:

> The Conservative Party is clearly identified in the minds of the electors with employers and big business, and they cannot deal objectively or fairly with the problems continually arising between employer and employee. The Labour Party is in the hands of the Trade Union Leaders.
> The return of a Socialist Government inevitably means that

> management is put on the defensive, for it does not know what is going to hit it next. The return of a Conservative Government means that the Trade Unions feel justified in going onto the offensive. The whole nation is the loser from this crazy line-up of power politics, and those who lose most in the struggle are those who live on fixed incomes, such as old age pensioners. (Liberal Manifesto, 1959)

This 'one nation' stance is a position that all major parties, in their attempt to appeal to the crucial middle ground of voters, have adopted. The image of pensioners as the deserving poor, which so dominates the party political thinking about older people, has both positive and negative effects. Insofar as old-age pensioners are in conflict with other groups in receipt of state-funded welfare, the very high level of legitimacy given to pensioners as deserving and poor serves to protect their interests. On the other hand, the images of passive older people as receivers of handouts for their past contribution to the nation prevents their being seen as a positive and active resource for society in the present.

One solution to dealing politically with both compassionate ageism and scapegoat ageism amongst the electorate (their desire to help the deserving poor and their fear of the costs) is presentational: be seen to do something but make sure it doesn't cost too much in the long term. Government initiatives such as the Better Government for Older People programme (a series of 'listening' events and pilot projects in collaboration with local councils and the major charities) and major publicity campaigns promoting benefits to older people might be seen as evidence of such an approach.

> One thing that is conspicuous is that this government has achieved very little in the areas which consistently come top of the pops for older people in political issue terms, like pensions, the National Health Service and so on. We see the government, which has rolled out quite a number of interesting things in the area of fuel poverty, trumpeting those from the rooftops in order to try and maintain that there has been action for older people. Somewhere just this week they launched the PR campaign to tell pensioners that they were going to get the winter fuel payment in November this year. They are going to get it automatically, it's going to drop through their letterboxes, but the government is still wanting to spend a two million advertising campaign on it. (Mervyn Kohler, Help the Aged, OPPOL interview)

Paul Flynn, a Labour MP, is also cynical about the government's actions. He believes that the government is very aware of the need to be seen to be looking after older people, and he states that this is the reason for well-advertised Christmas bonuses and fuel allowances:

What the government is doing is calculating what would seem to be acceptable and what this focus group say would be better. It's rather like the bad employer who cheats his worker every week in their wages and pays a lower wage and at Christmas time gives them a turkey. The perception of the value of the turkey is far greater than its value over the year, which might be two pence a week. (OPPOL interview)

How are Older People Perceived and What Are Our Responsibilities Towards Them?

'Poor Old Dears'

Pampel's (1998) concept of 'compassionate ageism' – older people being stereotyped as vulnerable and deserving – was certainly in evidence in our OPPOL focus group discussions. As Abigail, a participant in her early 30s, stated, 'We all, whether right or wrong, refer to a set of archetypes and there is a stereotypical old person, which is the person who is physically weak, and unsound of mind.' Older people were often described by interviewees as in need of care and assistance, dependent upon others and unable to look after themselves. There was much concern for the financial well-being of older people and interviewees unanimously agreed that something should be done to improve conditions for them.

> You hear of so many older people who don't put any heating on in the winter because it's too expensive and who don't put on any electricity. Christmas day they are sat in on their own and they've got no one to visit them and then they give them a TV licence! (Belinda, aged 29)

The focus group discussions highlighted the fact that older people's issues are very visible in the political arena. Participants were able to identify pensions, heating, crime and healthcare as important issues for the government to address. One older member of a focus group thought that older people's issues where high on the public agenda 'because they have the ability to put their cross' on the ballot paper (Bill, aged 52). This was rejected by another member of the group, who felt that it was older people's powerlessness, rather than their power, that brought their issues into the limelight:

> I think that the type of adverts that you see for Help the Aged or Age Concern or whatever portray older people as victims. You get a documentary on telly or whatever and the way that older people's issues are portrayed are like 'Oh, the poor old dear'. It's like if you're going to give them any attention or any thought, it's like when you're feeling sorry

for them. Whereas I think if you look at documentaries about young people, they are a lot more dramatic, a lot more drugs, sex and rock and roll. So you know, so there is a different kind of like reaction to issues that are around different ages. (Beth, aged 32)

Unlike support for other marginalised groups, support for the elderly is unquestionable. Older people would argue that the older generation fought in the war and not only contributed to but were the pioneers of the welfare state. The idea that people who fought in the war and paid contributions all their lives are now forced to live in poverty was abhorrent to most of the older people interviewed. Tom Moran, a leading Welsh pensioner activist now in his late 70s, was appalled when he realised that older people were so financially disadvantaged. It 'shook me, rocked me, men and women who had served their country, risked their lives, and now in their old age couldn't afford to buy a pint of beer in the Royal British Legion club – which sells beer at a remarkably cheap price'.

Younger people – although there was some sense that respect for the older generation was dissipating – acknowledged an inherent desire to look after the elderly. Laura, aged 31, put this very simply in a political context: 'If the government do things for the older generation it wins points with everyone because everyone's got a grandma.' Laura also felt that people look to the government to take responsibility for the elderly because families don't want to take responsibility for ageing relatives and feel they have been released from this role by modern political and cultural changes.

Successfully Retired Older People

Focus group participants admitted that when they thought of *older people*, they immediately thought of the dependent elderly. However there was some evidence that respondents were also aware of another group of older people in powerful positions.

There is undoubtedly a very senior citizen who is somewhat infirmed [sic] by the way that they are not able to really contribute positively in an economic sense. Then there is another older group, you know, those of us plus 50 through to 65–70 who are in many cases still in seats of power and able to work very positively and able to generate a return. (Bill, aged 52)

Others, especially younger participants, perceived older people as a group gaining wealth and attention at the expense of younger people. Laura, aged 31, felt that the elderly were a subject of too much concern: 'I don't see why people see the elderly as almost like helpless, I don't. I don't think that in a callous way. But I think that there are lots of other areas that are as important.' Her denial of being 'callous' is illustrative of the power of 'compassionate ageism' in setting expectations. Another participant, Abigail, also in her early 30s expressed her view as follows:

> When we talk about older people we have in mind a poor old pensioner who has hardly any money to live on, who freezes alone in her room and needs somebody to go and do the shopping for her, whereas there are older people who are also in corporate societies and other establishments. The older you are, the more money you get, which is scandalous in a way compared to young people who are, you know, scraping the bottom of the barrel.

On the other side of the coin some of the younger people we talked to spoke of older people's valuable contribution to society as volunteers and as carers for children whose parents both needed to work. One older person was concerned that older people were being abused as they effectively worked (at home) for nothing to increase the purchasing power of younger people.

In addition, there was a growing awareness amongst younger informants that elderly people are better off now than they ever were and of how this affects different age groups. Sarah, aged 23, said, 'I think there is a real difference in the age of the older people. You've got people that are, you know, now 65, 70, and a lot of them are reasonably rich. Newly retired people are fairly wealthy as are people who have worked after the war. Or you've got the people who are older than that who are fairly poor'.

A National Survey of Opinions

In order to gain some view of the generality of the ideas expressed by informants in the qualitative research with focus groups and interviewees, an opinion survey was commissioned from the polling organisation MORI. Details of the methodology were given in the Introduction to this book. Tables 8.1 to 8.5 below report the general findings. There are considerable methodological problems in combining qualitative and quantitative research. Qualitative research can reveal the complexity and range of opinion but seldom produces representative results. On the other hand, forcing people to choose one unqualified statement characterising older people as a group, as is typical of representative sample surveys, can elucidate the distribution of opinions but sacrifices a significant degree of validity. In the following sections, we describe the process of narrowing down the questions, as well as giving the numerical responses, in order to demonstrate the limitations of the data. Two initial questions were formulated for the national survey on older people's economic position. The first asked for one unqualified response to try to access people's 'gut response' to the question and to see whether people were willing to stereotype older people as a group. The second question gave some more qualified response options quoting from focus group discussions.

1. Please circle your most appropriate response to this statement.

Most pensioners are:

'rich'   'quite well off'   'making ends meet'   'poor'   don't know.

2. People discussing the increasing numbers of older people in the population have said the following things. Which one statement is closest to what you think? (Please circle one response only.)

'Older people are reasonably wealthy. They've worked all their lives and paid off their homes and can now use their retirement income to do whatever they want, be it going on expensive holidays, eating out or doing up their houses.'

'So many older people don't put any heating on in the winter because it's too expensive and don't put on any electricity. They sit in on their own most of the time and have no one to visit them.'

'Newly retired people are fairly wealthy. They are cool people now who get on with things, go sailing and water-skiing. But you've got the people who are older who are fairly poor and don't have enough money and aren't physically able to do anything but stay in and watch television.'

'Older people are at the time of their lives when they can enjoy life and don't have to worry about work. The state pension combined with occupational pensions and savings gives them enough money to live comfortably.'

None of the above.

However, people would have found it difficult to respond if they agreed with several of the statements, and the question might also be somewhat leading in terms of the statements selected. Further the financial constraints of the survey meant it was necessary to provide clear, short, mutually exclusive response options. Table 8.1 displays the question finally selected. Responses were interesting, but it is acknowledged that opinions regarding this are far more complex than can be represented in a survey.

On the issue of the perception of poverty, there is an indication that older people are still seen as not well off. Even though most of the people surveyed agreed that older people as a category contained both rich and poor people (66%), nearly a third of them (30%) still believed that older people generally were either quite poor or very poor.

Table 8.1 Opinions on poverty

In general, how rich or poor do you think most older people are?	
	%
Very rich	2
Some rich, some poor	66
Quite poor	27
Very poor	3
Don't know	2

Older People as Villains

Some elderly people are beginning to feel like villains in some sort of international plot to bring down the welfare state. In an OPPOL focus group Henrietta aged 76, who survives on the state pension alone, said:

> I do think you get to a stage where, it's better now, but we did go through a stage a little while ago about what it's going to cost to support all the elderly people in the country. It kept going on and on and I began to feel almost ashamed to be still alive.

Most younger people interviewed felt that an ageing population would cause problems for the distribution of welfare benefits and the National Health Service. Nigel, aged 36, was very concerned about how the government was going to fund an ageing population: 'The problem is the more old people get, the more money that has to be spent on health and things like that, and where is that money going to come from in the first place?'

Likewise, older people were also concerned about the dependency ratio. Dorothy, aged 73, said, 'I think it's hard on the next generation and the one after that – how are they going to manage to look after themselves and us older people?' However, her friend Harriet, aged in her 70s, felt that these kinds of fears where absurd, considering the quantity of national insurance paid by most older people over their years in employment. 'How are they going to manage? We've saved up for our old-age pension, we've worked all our lives!'

'There Just Isn't Enough Money'

The older people we interviewed were convinced that an increase in older voters didn't mean an increase in political power but rather the opposite. Myrtle, aged 72, expressed her views on the subject clearly: 'Politicians don't want to take on any causes for older people because there is so many of us, because whatever they do it will cost a lot of money.' Dorothy, aged 73, from another focus group, was in agreement: 'There is a higher proportion of older people in this country so they couldn't afford that.' Bill, aged 52, was pessimistic about the government's role in providing future pensions: 'There is no way that actually government can by itself provide the total pension requirement.' Younger people interviewed were convinced of the fact that there would not be a state pension in the future and that other welfare areas would be restricted. They suggested looking at less expensive ways of looking after older people, getting older people more involved in the voluntary sector and making older people fitter as ways of solving the problem.

If people generally believed that it would be impossible to support growing numbers of older people in an ageing population, then it would be possible to surmise that many of the political effects of compassionate ageism would be neutralised. It might be argued that policy makers would be seen to have a legitimate excuse for providing a restricted welfare regime. We used the survey to gain a nationally representative picture of opinions about the affordability of support for pensioners. We wanted to use original statements from the focus groups as possible survey responses to a question relating to the economic impact of an ageing population. The following statements used in our pilot survey seemed to best illustrate people's responses.

> People discussing the increasing numbers of older people in the population have said the following things. Which statement is closest to what you think? (Please circle one response only.)

> 'There are increasingly more older people in our population and therefore more money will have to be spent on health and pensions and things like that.'

> 'We can't afford to spend any more money on older people because there are so many of them, whatever we do will cost a lot of money, and the country just can't afford it.'

> None of the above.

> Don't know.

After piloting and discussion with MORI, it was agreed that a more simplified format needed to be used. Table 8.2 illustrates the question asked. The survey results make it clear that most people believe that the country can afford expanding welfare commitments. Seventy-three percent of those surveyed disagreed with the statement 'We can't afford to spend more money on older people because there are so many of them', although there was a substantial minority of around 17% who seemed to accept the arguments of demographic gloom.

Table 8.2 Opinions on affordability

To what extent do you agree with the following statement?
We can't afford to spend more money on older people because there are so many of them.

strongly agree	tend to agree	neither agree nor disagree	tend to disagree	strongly disagree	no opinion
3%	14%	9%	35%	38%	1%

From the Cradle to the Grave?

Most of the people we spoke to in our focus groups thought that older people should be looked after in their old age. People felt that everyone should have an equal right to healthcare and a pension although it was commonly expected that pensions would not be available in the future. There was a sense that concerns raised over the care of older people were not age-related issues but rather issues about citizenship.

> Not just older people – I think that that's just falsifying the issue. It's about state responsibility in general – as Cathie said, 'from cradle to the grave' and – it's part of their responsibility to look after people and to look after their needs, never mind their age. (Abigail, early 30s)

Belinda, from a younger persons' focus group, felt that the government purposely advertised policies and benefits for older people to get their votes because the electorate expects older people to be looked after:

> They [politicians] think they are doing what the rest of the country want for older people – to be paid for. So you will hear at Christmas, or you know everything will come on the telly about that ... and all the rest of it. (Belinda, aged 28)

Another female participant pointed out the fact that we have come to expect the government to take over the role of looking after the elderly, which was in the past, and in many other societies still is, the role of the family. It would take a major cultural shift for this role to be reintegrated into society, and it would not happen overnight.

> I think it's a real social issue. It's not about the government, it's not about money, it's about the way that our society has become. In other cultures it's different; they don't have a problem but the way that we live (and we are not the only culture), but we have become, one can say, too selfish. I think if the government cultivated a caring nation it would eliminate a lot of these problems. And it's not all about robbing from the students to give to the elderly; that's not what it's about because someone is always going to lose out. It's about changing a way of thinking. That's what it's about. It's not about moving money from A to B. (Laura, aged 31)

One group expressed the concern that, because these roles have been taken up by the government and/or other organisations, individuals and families have become complacent about older people.

> I think this is sort of like deferring responsibility. People can say, well, I'm not going to bother about so and so because... (Beth, aged 32)

> ....'That's the government's job.' (Stuart, aged 25)

> ....'I'll vote and the government can sort it out.' I think that kind of blinds people to not actually bothering to take responsibility. (Beth, aged 32)

Participants who worked in the voluntary sector and participate in their communities separated national and local issues. Whereas election policies are all about the financial role of the state, much of the care for older or disadvantaged people is provided at a local level. The role of older people themselves is crucial here, as a lot of the care and voluntary work is done by retirees.

> I think one of the things that's really important ... is to look at the difference between politics, in terms of national government, and like when people organise themselves at a community level, and I think something like politics, that tends to be about financial issues and power and status in terms of how much income you can earn, etc. Because I think at a localised community level that everybody is important, you know, that everybody's wisdom, historical perspective, everyone's potential contribution, is really important. (Beth, aged 32)

> It's maximising on the contribution. This place, this volunteer bureau, is indicative of that. It creates a place where people who have retired from

business activity can still come in and play a very important role in what's going on in this city. (Bill, aged 52)

That's right. We have 70-year-olds as well as very young people here involved in a variety of activities and it's this, the politics, where people look at their purse at the end of the week to see how much money they have got and therefore how important they are, and so on – and I think that's really leading away, as Beth pointed out, from what should be important, and that is rebuilding communities and where everybody has a say in it and has a role in it.... (Abigail, early 30s)

However, it was still considered that real care and responsibility for the elderly should lie with the government. The voluntary sector's role was considered invisible yet crucial by providing a backup to the government's inadequate performance as a carer.

I think there is a problem while you have really effective organisations like this because the government don't value [them], like volunteering, and a huge amount of volunteering occurs around older people. As that continues to be provided by volunteers, the government sees its role lessening to those groups because the value of it becomes lower because you always have people who are willing to help out. (Cathie, aged 25)

Yet there is a fear that if the responsibility is left to the government alone, it might not get taken care of:

I think that it's like giving to beggars in the street. Do you give to the beggar? If everyone gave to the beggar the government wouldn't have to do anything about it. But if you don't give to the beggar, the beggar's not going to eat that day. (Cathie, aged 25)

When looking specifically at the government's role concerning pensions, feelings ran high. Younger people felt that the government should provide for people in their old age but admitted to assuming that they would not have state pension provision when it came to their time to retire. In practice most younger people interviewed did not have pension plans. Most of the older people interviewed did have some extra pension provision but felt that the state pension wasn't enough and knew many people that struggled to live on it. The most interesting discussion about the government's role in pension provision occurred in a group in which ages ranged from 21 to 53 years. The younger people in this group argued that the government should take responsibility for pensions, whereas an older man in the group argued that people should take responsibility for their savings throughout their working life.

There is no way that actually government can by itself provide the total pension requirement and we all have to contribute towards it in whatever way we can depending on what level of salary one is on in your normal working life. (Bill, aged 52)

The younger people in the group felt that National Insurance should cover the cost of the pension. Bill, aged 52, thought that although people should get back their contributions, they shouldn't assume 'that they have this God-given right for the government to pay out if they've never saved themselves'. One younger woman said she would consider placing her vote with a government who promised to ensure her a pension in the future because she thought the government should take this role seriously. The argument continued, questioning whether the government was an adequate financial manager to control these monies. This seemed to be something the younger people in the group hadn't thought about before.

If it's all just government gets it and you don't really see what they are doing with it.... (Beth, aged 32)

It gives you control over your money if you do it privately. (Bill, aged 52)

Well I would have absolutely no trust in any private company over a period of time. Because they can go down, they can go bust. Anything can happen to them and I really would not. I think it really should be a safeguard. (Abigail, early 30s)

Well what about a swinging government? I mean, you go from one party to the next. Total policies get reversed over night. Then you've got no guarantee with the government. The pressures on the government, the economics of maintaining the infrastructure of the country and everything else. Are you guaranteed your pension through that? (Bill, aged 52)

The whole thing about private pensions – I think what the government ought to be providing is some sort of comprehensive advice for people looking to take out pension policies, because the main reason I haven't done anything about it is that I don't trust any company because I don't know anything about them. If I wanted to get a private pension, I haven't got a clue where to start. (Cathie, aged 25)

The main thing that emerged from these discussions was that participants felt that if indeed the government isn't going to take responsibility for pensions, then it needs to provide adequate advice and some type of fallback plan so that nobody would be left destitute.

There was clear evidence to suggest that the public will hold governments accountable for the care of older people. The majority of the people surveyed in the MORI poll (65%) agreed that the working population should look after older people financially.

Table 8.3 Opinions on financial support

To what extent do you agree with the following statement?
The working population should support older people financially.

strongly agree	tend to agree	neither agree nor disagree	tend to disagree	strongly disagree	no opinion
24%	41%	14%	15%	5%	1%

How Do Older People Perceive Themselves and Their Political Power?

'Putting Their Cross'

An ageing population may indeed put strain on the resources needed to support older people, but it will also mean that there are more older people in the electorate potentially prepared to protect these resources with their vote. Many older people see this as a strength of the ageing population.

> The very fact that so many people are living that much longer. That is a huge element of the voting community and government is very much aware of that. (Bill, aged 52)
>
> Interviewer: Do you think so?
>
> I think so. Because they are all going to go out and put their cross. They find that one party is actually going to support greater emphasis towards the older generation, then people are going to go to that party.

It was generally agreed in the focus group discussions that most older people vote and that they are far more interested in using their right to vote than younger people are. Many of the younger people were disillusioned or disinterested in voting and politics. They were described by one 23-year-old woman as unfashionable. It was commented that they are not discussed in younger people's arenas, such as school or popular magazines. A younger man said that he kept abreast of news and regularly read the newspapers but said he didn't believe in politics and turned the page straightaway if he saw politics in the newspapers. Citizenship and voting were simply not as important to the younger participants as it appeared to be to the older ones.

> I think that older people are far more likely to go out and vote because it's

just not, I mean it's quite interesting ... but citizenship and voting has not been drummed into me. Not once at school did I do anything about voting at all ... It was never discussed. It was like it's not really our thing. (Cathie, aged 25)

Consequently younger people's reactions to the concept of compulsory voting, which is policy in Australia, was quite different to that of older people. (The group facilitator was Australian.) The younger people were definitely against the concept of compulsory voting, whereas the older ones were quite the opposite although, ironically, it seems clear that compulsion is not needed to get older people to the polling booths.

I always vote. I've voted all the way round the clock, as it were. I do think it's a very important part of democracy. (Bert, aged in his 70s)

The older people interviewed felt it to be their responsibility to vote, and considered voting a right that should not be taken for granted.

But if you don't participate, then you cannot complain or criticise, which, regrettably, people do. If we are going to live in a social group in a community, in a society, then everyone has a responsibility to be involved in the process of that society. (Bill, aged 52)

I would guess that quite a lot of older people do vote, because we've always been responsible, because particularly as women we feel that women fought to get us the vote. Therefore we do have a duty and a responsibility and because, being older, most of us associate rights with responsibilities. I think that one of the troubles is that nowadays a great many people are very happy to assume their rights but they don't want to take responsibility. (Myrtle, aged 72)

However, a few older people, who would never consider not voting, questioned the effectiveness of their vote.

I have voted at every possible election since I've been at the age of 18 and I missed one which I couldn't get to and I have very strong feelings that the effectiveness of your voting on what happens is diminishing. I feel that the value of my vote decreases because I think the parliamentarians go their own way regardless, today to a much greater extent. Really they should be coming to the people of the country and getting an opinion from you and the opinion is represented by how you vote. I think today they come to the people of the country but it is a less effective conveying of your opinions and wishes. Whips, parliamentary parties tend to go the way they want. Once they are in power they forget about the voters and tend to go very much their own way. (Graham, aged in his 70s)

Yes, in a way I don't think that we are always voting for our own opinions because we can pick points from each political party where we agree and we could also pick points from each political party where we disagree, but you've only got a chance to vote for one or the other. You can't express the whole of your opinion over a very wide field by a single vote. So we're really governed by what the individual political parties' programmes are. Part of which you might agree, most people would disagree with some part of it. (Bert aged in his 70s)

One male participant in a mixed-gender older person's focus group expressed the concern that although older people should have strong voting power, policies still do not reflect this.

What I can't understand is, here we are supposed to have a very high proportion of elderly people. They've got some sense of voting power, they've got some strong pull behind them, and yet we don't seem to be able to do anything with it. (Malcolm, aged 69)

When asked whether voting gave them a say in the running of the country, respondents said that it wasn't a perfect system but it remained the main way that they could express themselves to politicians.

It's the only method that we've got at the moment. I mean we may not like it, there may be a lot of weaknesses to it and a lot of problems, but it's the only system that we've got. I think that very point that you made about the participation by more females in power, the ethnic minorities and so on – that has come about because those people have stood up and they have gone forward. They have put their cross on the piece of paper. (Bill, aged 52)

Voting for Self Interest?: 'I'm all right Jack'

Well, I think I'll write to my MP and remind him that the number of older people is getting greater and he better watch it. (Malcolm, aged 69)

Despite this sentiment most older people do not feel themselves to have voted out of self-interest. However, many of the younger people we interviewed felt that an ageing population would mean that older people's issues would begin to dominate the political agenda.

Once again that's getting back to the age thing. The older people are taking the initiative there because younger people don't have the time or can't be bothered. So you are once again getting a swing towards what the older people want, not what the cross-section of the population wants. (Noel, aged 25)

The trend may have passed over the last couple of years, older people may have looked a little bit more closely at the policy rather than just sticking with the party line, so I think they are probably voting more because they have a more valid judgement. Older people, a wiser view of it. I think that what concerns me is that if more and more older people actually do vote and less and less younger people vote, the policies.... (Keith aged 40)

A few older people agreed with this. John, aged 77, saw it as a fairly simplistic fact. 'It will eventually, I suppose, – the ratio will be wrong, won't it? In the end you'll get so many older people that we will have too much of an influence like, that the youngsters won't be listened to.' Yet most older people either didn't think the government would listen to them because there would not be enough money to meet their needs or were not prepared to vote on age-related issues. The following discussion with a group of women in their 70s illustrates older people's reluctance to vote according to age related issues.

Do you think older people will start to vote as a block? (Interviewer)

I would rather vote on my own ... [inaudible].

It's the larger picture we are voting for, isn't it? (Kate)

I don't want to vote for older people ... 'I'm all right Jack' but I do feel that something should be done about the youngsters; there should be jobs. (Harriet)

What you are doing is articulating arguments on behalf of younger people, on behalf of unemployed people.... (Interviewer)

Yes. (Kate)

Yes, not ourselves. (Harriet)

Likewise, any lobbying on behalf of older people is seen to be competing for resources with other disadvantaged groups, such as children or the disabled. When Mrs L was asked whether she would vote for someone who offered a good deal for pensioners, she said, 'I would shy away from that if he was just on about doing something for pensioners. It would get the youngsters' backs up. You've got to have a balanced thing, appeal to everybody'.

A few younger respondents with grandparents themselves also thought that older people would be more likely to look after their grandchildren's interests than their own.

I think cost of living is what older people ... that's what my gran was really ... and their children, a lot of people do worry about their children a lot and what's going to happen. (Sarah, aged 23)

Well, what's the agenda of the older person? Because if you've got children or grandchildren, you'd want to do the best for them, wouldn't you? (Jim, aged 36)

Many of the people who, when first questioned, felt that an ageing population would have an impact on politics, changed their minds on further questioning, admitting that older people would be unlikely actively to seek to put pressure on the government to improve their situations.

Um, what difference do I think it will make to politics? Well, I was thinking the other day, I don't know what happens with MPs, how long they serve, whether we will have a higher proportion of older MPs. I think they'll be forced to consider the issues that matter to the people who are retired or going towards retirement. I think they'll be forced to by the sheer numbers of the population that are retired. (Beryl, aged 58)

How will that force them? (Interviewer)

Good God, I don't really know. (Beryl)

Do you think older people will vote more as a block and get things passed? (Interviewer)

I'd like to think so, but I think it depends how well they are, you know, whether they are apathetic or have got used to being ignored. No, I don't think so. I mean I'm trying to compare myself with my mother, who opts out of everything. She doesn't have an enquiring mind at all. (Beryl)

Voting for Generational Interests

As a generation, older people, it appeared, were very concerned about issues surrounding national identity. All of the older people's focus groups brought up issues regarding national identity as issues they felt were important for the government to address. They expressed very strong feelings about the disadvantages of devolution, and the European Union, which they felt threatened not only national identity but also British power to legislate for itself. The discussion reproduced below between members of the older women's focus group illustrates the strength of opinions expressed about devolution:

I'm very worried about this fact that we are splitting up. My grandfather was a Scot, my daughter-in-law is a Scot, I was brought up in Wales. I'm a London cockney. I'm British. On my passport it says 'British'. I don't want to be English. I want to be British. (Harriet, aged in her 70s)

Well, I'm British as well, but when people ask me, I say I'm English. I was born and bred in London and all my family are English – do you know what I mean? (Kate, aged in her 70s)

But if Scotland splits away from the UK and Ireland already has, and then it will be Wales, then it will be Cornwall. (Penelope, aged in her 70s)

I think that if they are going to be divided from us, I don't think they should have a say in what goes on in England. (Mary, aged in her 70s)

Another focus group participant from the mixed gender group expressed concerns that funds were being redirected from England into the newly devolved assemblies.

More of our national income has gone into supporting Scotland and Wales than it has in England. And I do begin to think, well, when are the English going to have some say? But until recently I've never thought of myself as English. I just thought of myself as British. And I think this is just making us more nationalistic. (Henrietta, aged 76)

An older man felt that the strength of feeling regarding the European issue would really make a difference at the polling booths.

I think if a country as a whole feels a thing, it does eventually get through to the politicians. It will influence the politicians into doing what the country wants, but it's a long, hard slog, very difficult to get over, and there has to be terrific unanimity within the country. To give a little example, I think the present government plan to take us into Europe lock stock and barrel, and they really pitched themselves on a referendum and the result of that referendum would be to say 'no, we are not going into Europe,' and they've had to stall on this. And now that's where the majority of the country feel that joining the Euro financially would be a bad thing and we have crossed Mr Blair and his party's wishes on this. I think the feeling is so strong that they have deferred it and put it off, and I think their chances of getting this are getting weaker by the month. So, yes, I think massive strong feeling gets through, but if Joe has got a little hobby horse he doesn't have a hope in hell. (Graham, aged in his 70s)

One younger woman also brought this up as an important issue, but it seemed that it was definitely an issue of importance expressed by all of the older people we spoke to.

People in Brussels are making decisions for our country. I just don't think that's right. (Sarah, aged 23)

We wanted to obtain a general idea of people's impressions about the political power of older people in an ageing population through the use of the national survey. The statements below were used in our pilot survey and covered the range of opinions that people gave during focus groups:

People discussing the increasing numbers of older people in the population have said the following things. Which statement is closest to what you think? (Please circle one response only.)

'If the proportion of older people grows and they're not treated properly, then their vote is going to influence the government. The government is going to say "We'll have to pay attention to their needs, otherwise they'll get us thrown out".'

'Politicians can't take on any causes for older people because there is so many of them. Whatever they do will cost a lot of money, and the country just can't afford it.'

'Older people aren't like truck drivers. They can't go on strike or block the motorways so governments won't take any notice of them no matter how many of them there are.'

'If older people stand together and put pressure on the government the government will have to listen to them and increase their pensions and health benefits.'

'It doesn't matter who is in power or how many older people there are, older people's issues are never going to be high on the political agenda.'

'Older people can make a difference at a local level on a parish council sort of scheme of things. But on the wider national picture, I don't think they have or will ever have that much influence.'

'The more older people we get, the more money will have to be spent on health and pensions and things like that, because people expect the government to look after older people.'

It did not prove a practical possibility to explore on a representative basis the complexity of opinions. Respondents' ideas about older people's political power were varied and complex, but large-scale national polling precludes complexity, and it is methodologically unsound to ask respondents to choose one response in a survey from a set of responses that are not mutually exclusive. The questions asked in the survey were simplified and appear in Tables 8.4 and 8.5.

Most people surveyed believed that if older people put pressure on the government, then the government would increase its spending on older people. Sixty-three percent of respondents agreed that 'if older people campaigned together, then the government would have to increase spending on pensions and health'. Yet 62% agreed that older people's issues were never going to be high on the political agenda (see Vincent, Patterson and Wale, 2000, for a detailed discussion of these findings).

Table 8.4　Opinions on campaigning

To what extent do you agree with the following statement?
If older people campaigned together then the government would have to increase spending on pensions and health.

strongly agree	tend to agree	neither agree nor disagree	tend to disagree	strongly disagree	no opinion
21%	42%	13%	17%	5%	2%

Table 8.5　Opinions on the political agenda

To what extent do you agree with the following statement?
Older people's issues are never going to be high on the political agenda.

strongly agree	tend to agree	neither agree nor disagree	tend to disagree	strongly disagree	no opinion
20%	42%	12%	20%	4%	2%

Conclusion: Dangerous Pressure Group or Deserving Poor?

> Pressure groups are effective because it is people who have economic activity and power, because they can go on strike and so on, whereas older people are just a bunch of individuals who cost us a lot. (Abigail, aged in her 30s)

It might well be that an ageing population has forced governments to think again about adequate provision for the elderly, although it seems more likely that an ageing population is providing the means by which politicians can justify a decreased responsibility for welfare. Our focus groups unanimously agreed that the welfare system couldn't cope with an ageing population; there is just not enough money left in the pot. If the general consensus were that governments have very little financial ability to change the circumstances of older people, then, it would appear, older people's interests could be effectively marginalised.

Older people are a very diverse set of people and their material conditions are widely varied. The focus group discussions acknowledged this increasing diversity, especially the fact that the younger pensioners benefiting from occupational pensions are not as badly off as previous generations of older people. Figures would suggest that it is people past their 70s, who missed out on occupational pensions, who are experiencing most financial difficulty. However, it is these people whom our focus group participants were most concerned about. There was a real sense of indignation about the maltreatment of older people in society that was stirred up within the focus groups by the participants themselves. There was really little evidence of scapegoat ageism. The participants said we should look after older people *and* they said that we cannot afford to look after the elderly in the future. They did not say that we should look after the elderly *but* we cannot afford to anymore so we will not. There was not a sense that older people were the cause of or were to blame for the situation. Rather, there was a sense of resignation that the moral commitments were difficult to live up to.

There was an indication that older people collectively are still seen as not particularly affluent. Even though most of the people surveyed (66%) agreed that older people as a category contained both rich and poor people, nearly a third (30%) still believed that older people generally were either quite poor or very poor. There was also clear evidence to suggest that the public will hold governments accountable for the care of older people. The majority (65%) agreed that we should look after older people financially, and it was made clear that most people believe that the country can afford to meet its welfare commitments. Seventy-three percent of those surveyed *disagreed* with the statement 'We can't afford to spend more money on older people because there are so many of them'. However, despite this, people generally appeared to question the idea that politicians will place importance on older people's issues. Sixty-two percent agreed that older people's issues were never going to be high on the public agenda. Yet most people believed that if older people put pressure on the government, it would increase spending on older people. Sixty-three percent of respondents agreed that 'if older people campaigned together, then the government would have to increase spending on pensions and health'.

These opinions suggest that, rather than older people's self-interested votes being the significant key political factor, it is the attitudes of the general population that matter most. The attitudes held by the general public constrain the political options of parties and governments. First, there is evidence to suggest that the public expect the government to continue to meet the needs of older people regardless of expanding welfare commitments. The survey also established that the great majority of the electorate believe that there should be collective provision for older people. Governments who are seen to fail to look after the older section of the population can expect a reaction from the general population.

The general public do think that older people as a group would be able, if they got together, to put pressure on the government to improve their own circumstances. The significance of this opinion is debatable. It could well be that respondents were merely expressing a generalised belief in democracy and that the larger number of voters ought to prevail. The survey also found that 62% of respondents felt that older people's issues were never going to be high on the government's agenda. This opinion may reflect respondents' realistic expectations of contemporary politics. Age group issues are not the predominant issues by which elections are won and lost; historically, older people have not voted out of self-interest, and our focus group responses suggest that this is unlikely to change. However, generational differences in opinion on specific issues that affect the nation as a whole arose in the focus group discussions reported above. These specific issues are where older people are more likely to exert influence at the polls.

An examination of the opinions and electoral preferences of older voters as opposed to those of the middle-aged or young suggest that electoral strategies addressed to them, as older people, will not be successful. They do not see age categories to be significant and follow the dominant culture in valuing newness, youth and a sense of community. Older voters feel a sense of social responsibility and have a community pride in the welfare state and the NHS. For the 'war' generation, national pride is based on a particular set of shared experiences, most importantly as young people between 1939 and 1945. This generation both fought the war and established the welfare state. It may be that the increasingly anti-Europe stance of the Conservatives plays well with older people, who are less internationally oriented than younger people and value national cohesion more than they do. These issues of generation and politics will be explored in the next chapter.

9 Citizenship and Generation

Introduction

The issues underlying the contemporary politics of old age in Britain are citizenship and generation. Symbols of a generation are more important to a sense of solidarity than are manifestations of age. Fellow-feeling stems from common experience, not arbitrary age criteria. To some, senior citizenship is experienced as a form of second-class citizenship. Hence the focus in this study on the issues associated with the future of the welfare state. The status and future of the British state pension are uncertain, as is the future direction of the welfare system itself. Over the last twenty years of the twentieth century there has been increasing public debate about the need for individuals to prepare for old age through personal private pension schemes.

Older people are often very forthright in their argument for the retention of the basic values that informed the creation of the welfare state. They are also particularly vulnerable to the indignities that await people should the welfare state and the national health system fail them. Employing ethical arguments that appeal to social justice within a national community, they use slogans reflecting their fundamental belief in both democracy and a national health system. 'We fought to defend democracy from Hitler' is a common refrain among not only those who served in the armed forces in the Second World War but those who participated on the 'home front'. 'We struggled to get a state pension and to build up the National Health Service and the welfare state' is another. The current generation of older people make the moral link between citizenship and the pension, associating the sacrifices of defending the nation and contributing to its freedoms and economic success with the right to a basic retirement income. Does social citizenship have a future, or is it merely the nostalgia of a dying generation?

Citizenship and the Future of the Welfare State

At the centre of any contemporary discussion about citizenship, there is a debate about the proper role of the state in providing income security, and health and social care for its citizens. There is a sense amongst most people in Britain that health, welfare and pensions should be to some considerable extent the responsibility of the state (Williams et al., 1999; Hayden et al., 1999). Healthcare and the pension are seen as citizenship rights, but there are serious concerns about the future of these rights. The concept 'citizenship' has important connotations for older people. There are substantial and growing differentials in the experience of being old. Studies, including Midwinter (1991) and Walker and Maltby (1997:17) suggest that less well-off older people prefer the term 'senior citizen', while the relatively better-off prefer to be referred to as a 'retired'. The former presumably prefer the term 'citizen' because it emphasises people's rights in the mutuality of the state and legitimate access to benefits that flow from a lifetime of fulfilling the duties of a citizen (although they might not express those sentiments in such language). The label 'retired', on the other hand, implies a history of work and its rewards. It is also possible to speculate that there is a gender difference embedded in this data. In general, older women have different experiences of household labour, are less likely to have good employment-related pensions and overall are more likely to experience poverty in old age than men. Shunning the identity of the 'deserving poor' – suitable cases for charity – older people prefer to be seen as common members of a national community who expect a pension on retirement and care in old age by virtue of having shouldered the duties of citizenship.

Many leading campaigners deplore the extent to which the pensioners' movement has become exclusively organised by and for older people. For Barbara Castle, Bruce Kent and others, there should not be a *senior* citizens' movement but a citizens' movement. Since becoming a pensioner, Bruce Kent has taken the podium many times backing the movement's push to restore the link between earnings and pensions. He regrets the extent to which the pensions issue has become exclusively an issue for pensioners.

> My vision would be that everybody reads up about the first pensioners' campaign and see how very different it was ... It was not a campaign organised by pensioners. It emerged from a sense of national injustice about what was being done to one section of the community and that sense of injustice was experienced by all sorts of people ... I don't know how or if it ever came to voting decisions, but it was certainly open to all ages. They wouldn't have known what it meant to say 'only pensioners'. But the pensioners' campaign today is in the hands of pensioners – like at Manchester, you have two hundred people over the age of 65 in a room. It's not a national indignity. You don't have a vivisection campaign with the only concerned people [those] who've experienced cruelty to animals. (Bruce Kent, OPPOL interview)

History of Citizenship as Political Rights

The history of citizenship is the history of the nation-state, and there is an abundant and disciplinarily diverse literature on the subject (for example, Steenbergen, 1994; Barbalet, 1988; Twine, 1994). Guibernau (1996), amongst others, states that it is usual to locate the rise of nation-state and nationalism in late eighteenth century Europe and to link their emergence to the ideas that gave rise to the American Revolution in 1776 and the French Revolution in 1789. The rise of the nation-state involved a complex change in the relations of power in society and a fundamental shift in the ideologies that legitimated the ruling institutions.

> Before the eighteenth century, the right to rule was legitimated by appeal to God's will, royal blood or superior physical strength and these reasons were premised upon the belief that legitimacy came from above, rather than from the rules. A radical shift occurred as a consequence of the spread of the new ideas of the *philosophes* emphasising the cult of liberty, equality and particularly the idea of state power rooted in popular consent. (Guibernau, 1996:52)

The developments in political thought in the eighteenth century elaborated the idea of citizenship and saw the drafting of constitutions that granted equality before the law. These dominant ideas meant that states found it necessary to generate schemes for regulating the rights and duties of their citizens. The way people were to be governed was, in ideal terms, conducted through universalistic criteria rather than based on personal favour or privilege. Legal-rational authority was the basis of bureaucratic allocation of rights and duties by age. National systems for birth and death registration were required in order to administer duties, such as conscription and taxation, and rights, such as child benefit and pensions.

Tarrow (1994), amongst others, sees the development of the nation-state in terms of a power struggle. He argues that by the second half of the nineteenth century, the power of social movements, and their potential for disruption, had led national states to broaden the suffrage, accept the legitimacy of mass associations and open up new forms of participation to their citizens. Citizenship emerged through a rough dialectic between social movements – actual or feared – and the national state. In the twentieth century the nation-state became almost synonymous with society. Mann (1988) suggests that as class struggles became regulated and institutionalised, nations emerged and classes developed a certain loyalty to the nation. So in the first half of the twentieth century the middle and working-classes became national citizens, and were prepared to work and fight to defend the symbols of their citizenship – monarch, flag, homeland and kith and kin. Mann, discussing the First World War, says:

> The war became a 'people's war' and the people wanted victory even at the cost of slaughter. The people were somewhat isolated from the front (except in France) and did not appreciate its full devastation. But also, the experience of the middle class before the war – progress through the nation – now became more generalised to the people as a whole. The people sacrificed but not for nothing. A bargain was struck, fairly explicitly: at the end of the war there would be extension of the franchise (probably including women) and welfare reforms. The downpayment was made already: full employment and greater trade union rights. The entry of the working class, and of women, into citizenship was accelerated by mass mobilization warfare. (Mann, 1988:157-158)

The period immediately following the Second World War saw the foundation and elaboration of the welfare state in Britain. Originally published in 1950, the work of T.H. Marshall is frequently used to set out the rhetoric of social citizenship (Marshall, 1992). Marshall's account of citizenship was not just a theory, but a justification of postwar governments that pursued social democratic policies. Marshall's model of citizenship can be seen as providing a basis for integrating individuals and classes within the wider community. It was an optimistic formulation based on the idea that in Britain there had been a historical progression of freedom, moving from civil to social rights between the eighteenth and twentieth centuries (Marshall, 1992). That postwar Britain represented the triumph of social development was taken as read (Titmus, 1974). The inequalities created though the Industrial Revolution and the market were to be contained by the state in order to establish social harmony. Citizens were to have a stake in society, one which removed the desire to change radically the institutional order or to challenge the centrality of the market (Higgs, 1998:118).

The history of citizenship and the state influences the attitudes of generations. There is a pre-war generation, which has family memories of the workhouse and of the impact of the means test on the unemployed during the Great Depression. Attitudes to means testing and the significance and meaning of means tests vary with cohort experience and collective memory (Hussey, 1999). Similarly, the postwar generation's attitudes carry the imprint of the success of social citizenship and the creation of the welfare state. Those who experienced the Second World War and then the postwar boom, together with the triumph of social democracy, form a distinctive cohort. The impact of those ideas and values are still reflected in the current attitudes of that Second World War generation. This cohort/generation are now today's older people and see the changes in health and welfare from this perspective. Those who were in their 20s in the 1950s are now in their 70s. Those born 1920-1930, who were between 20 and 30 in 1950 and are now between 70 and 80, are the war generation, to whom these values are particularly important.

Below are some responses to a question from a postal survey of Devon pensioners of this generation (Age Concern Exeter, 1999):

> What improvements would you most like to see in the Health Service or Social Services over the next 30 years?

> 'Less mixed sex beds in wards (none), longer recovery time – overnight after ops. Increase income tax to help pay health services. Remember, we have worked all our lives, and paid our National Health Stamp. I was a nurse for years and my husband served in the RAF in Burma 5 years!' (Widow over 70 from South Devon)

> 'As I am elderly, how many years have I to worry over? I am content as I am. But as we, the elderly, have had our lives altered by the loss of husbands, in war and peace; we paid for all this care, and really should be a form of priority....' (Widow over 70 from Mid-Devon)

The history of citizenship is then the history of the nation-state. The nation-state, in the form of the post-Second World War social democratic states, formed a historically specific compromise between capital and labour. The challenge, which such welfare states tried to meet, was to provide for all citizens equally. However, it is clear from subsequent critiques of Marshall that, in practice, groups of second-class citizens persisted and new ones arose. Higgs provides a clear, comprehensive overview of the issues and comes to some insightful conclusions about the prognosis for citizenship (Higgs, 1997:118-131). He suggests that there are a range of theoretical criticisms that can be directed at Marshall's account of citizenship, highlighting issues such as its historical accuracy (Rees, 1996), its Anglo-centrism (Mann, 1987) and its failure to acknowledge the importance of conflict (Giddens, 1982). He argues that a significant flaw was to overlook the gendering of citizenship that was implicit in the original design (Pedersen, 1993), which resulted in the failure to establish women's social needs as rights. The conflation of nationality with citizenship is another aspect of Marshall's account that was seemingly unproblematic at the time but that has become of central concern to politics since the 1960s (Rees, 1996). This problem of the nature of citizenship seems to lie at the centre of current dilemmas on the future of health and welfare provision. Who precisely is entitled to claim equal access to health and welfare on the basis of citizenship?

Older voters feel a sense of national community, and part of that community pride lies with the welfare state and the NHS in particular. However, these attitudes can be 'populist'; the sense of community can be manifested as antagonism to outsiders and deviants. Scroungers are deplored; older people want the community of the welfare state, but are deeply antagonistic to others whom they see as unfairly taking advantage of it. These attitudes can be linked to a reluctance to take up benefits and to accept labels derived from the benefits system – the identity as a welfare recipient is rejected. The response of citizenship theory to the postmodern diversity and plurality of identity has been the proliferation of new citizenships. The debate over the rights of gay people to marry and to have legitimate children illustrates one of a wide and diverse range of citizenship claims. Isin and Wood (1999) list, in addition to civil, political and social citizenship, 'diasporic and aboriginal citizenship', 'sexual citizenship', 'cosmopolitan citizenship', 'cultural citizenship' and 'radical citizenship' in their chapter titles. There are serious problems with proliferating this list still further (see for example Roche, 1995). However, to advance the argument, we will demonstrate that there are also people who are second-class citizens by virtue of their age.

Older People's Identity and Citizenship

> Old people are not lesser beings. (Woman over 80 responding to Age Concern's Millennium Debate of the Age in Devon)

People are excluded from specific citizens' rights and duties (for example, jury service, certain health treatments and certain tax and welfare benefits) on the basis of their age. State bureaucracies and other regulatory systems limit access to the supply of commodities by age. Age-based regulations structure access to tobacco, subsidised rail and bus travel, television licences and so on. The *Guardian* (8 November 1999) reports an Age Concern survey which indicates that a significant proportion of older people believe they are excluded by their age from some healthcare treatments. Pensioners' groups campaign against discrimination in healthcare and seek to reveal the structure of administrative regulation that limits older people's consumption of health services. The following exchange illustrates the belief that age discrimination in healthcare occurs:

> Now a lot of people and me personally are very concerned about healthcare. Am I, when I go to my doctors and present a particular problem, going to get medication, the hospital appointment and the treatment that I need for it? Or are they going to look at me and say, well, she's 62 – she can have x, y, z because we won't give her what she needs or the treatment because of her age? (Mrs C., aged 62, OPPOL interview)

Do you think that really happens? (Interviewer)

I have a sneaky feeling that it does happen, because resources are limited and they will target the people that they think it will benefit the most, and I think that can be quite a scary thought. I recently said to my son, 'If ever I became ill or incapacitated, I think you will have to stand up and fight for me.' (Mrs C.)

Yes, we had someone in earlier who was saying a similar sort of thing about her husband who was elderly and she had to really push to get him some treatment. (Interviewer)

I lost my husband last year with a heart attack in the car and he'd had a slight heart attack in December. It was discovered in his post mortem that his arteries had narrowed, etc. etc. and my son was terribly upset because he said 'if they had of given Dad this "endioplas"' or something, he said, 'You know, we could have paid for it. If they just said he needed it.' He said, 'Our money was there and we could have paid for it. He could have had it.' But I don't think so. I think the damage was done, and I think if they had have done it, even then the outcome would probably have been the same. But he personally felt and still feels that he was cheated and lost his dad when we had the money and could of paid for it. And I think there must be a lot of people like your lady there who is watching a loved one who is being denied, perhaps treatment, because of costs when you get to a certain age. (Mrs C.)

Older people experience an unwelcome loss of full citizenship that they and others feel needs to be addressed. There is as yet no specific legal requirement in the UK not to discriminate on the basis of age.[38] There are two aspects to this diminished status, citizenship by age and citizenship by generation. There is an identity that is generated by people's sense of their own and others' longevity. The internalisation of such sentiments is expressed in the statement 'You only know what it is like to be old when you have lived as long as I have.' There is also a different identity that is generated by a sense of common historical experience felt by a cohort: 'Those of us who went through the war know what is like to have to stick together.' In practice, of course, these identities are closely tied to one another. However, they also lead to claims for full and special citizenship, citizenship that encompasses rights and duties accumulated over a lifetime, or in specific historical circumstances.

Claims made by groups to an authentic identity are derived from common experience. Pronouncements are frequently made following the

---

[38] In practice, European legislation and the enactment of human rights legislation in the UK are potentially establishing legal remedies for age discrimination.

general pattern of 'We are a real group, and you would know this had you lived the same experiences as us' or 'You don't know what it is like unless you are a woman/black/working-class/Jewish/disabled/gay/Serb etc.' These claims to authentic experience are also claims for independence or autonomy by the group. They justify why others should not legislate for them. Those who do not share the same experiences, it is claimed, cannot therefore fully understand or represent the group. Older people can (and some do) claim to be an authentic special group by reference to both their age in years and their specific place in the nation's history. Cohort experience, that is common, lived-through history, can provide authentication of identity. The generation that is united by its experience of the Great Depression and the Second World War has been discussed above. The experience of longevity can also be used as a resource for self-identity. Accumulation of life history, having more experience of life simply by having lasted longer, is of course an inherent characteristic of older people. Duration, therefore, has consequences for identity. Identity can be linked to those experiences of life that necessarily require the passing of years, such as grandparenthood, great-grandparenthood, or the acquisition of grey hair, wrinkles or other physical markers of old age.

Sense of national identity, the scope of the national community and sense of citizenship as a moral and legal entity have changed through the course of the twentieth century. Aspects of biography and of cohort historical experience will shape the identity of an older person and the meaning and role of citizenship in his or her identity. Knowledge and understanding of citizenship is age-related. It is worth emphasising that the war generation have a specific understanding of citizenship derived from their historical experience. Are ideas about citizenship also generation-related? It has been suggested that 'baby-boomers' will have a distinctive approach to old age. Is the idealisation of the market (with the 'consumer' as the desirable model of the citizen) a 'Thatcher's children' view of the world? What about Blair's babies – what will be their model of citizenship for succeeding generations?

Legitimacy and the Welfare State

There is a widespread distrust of and alienation from politics and politicians in contemporary Britain. Older people in general share the wider public's low opinion of politicians (Heath and Taylor, 1999). One possible source of this alienation, it can be argued, is the weakness of the nation-state in a globalised world (Mlinar, 1992). It can be argued that, irrespective of the effectiveness of the political process in articulating the will of the people and enabling them to influence decision making, there is a severe reduction in the ability of our current political institutions to deliver access to health and welfare to its citizens (Mishra, 1999). The imperatives of national competitiveness in the international marketplace ensure that individual countries cannot step too far out of line with taxation or insurance regimes. To do so, it is argued, would jeopardise their access to finance capital and a highly qualified workforce, and would price goods out of export markets. Therefore, the power of people in practice to change the distribution of health services and welfare benefits declines, with a consequent loss of a sense of political efficacy among the electorate. Older people do not seem to be able to exercise political power through the ballot box to achieve full and equal status in their access to healthcare and welfare. It is an irony that there is a clear generational difference in attitudes to political participation and the belief in the obligations of citizen participation in democracy. Older people express a much stronger belief in the obligation to vote and participate, whereas citizenship is less important to younger people (Vincent, Patterson and Wale, 2000).

There is a crisis of legitimacy for contemporary political institutions. The 16th British Social Attitudes survey conducted in 1999 reports that only a third of under-25-year-olds believed voting was a civic obligation. This contrasted with about two-thirds of 25-55-year-olds and 80% of people 65 and over. Over 30% of teenagers have 'no interest at all' in politics (Park, 1999). This extract from an OPPOL focus group of young people discussing politics and old age illustrates this crisis:

> I just don't believe in politics (Noel, aged 25)

[Laughter]

When asked if he read the paper, Noel answered:

> Yeah, but if I see politics I turn over straightaway....

And later in the session:

> It's that whole thing, isn't it? You're one voice – what the hell can you do against international politics?

Again in the same focus group from another member:

> The reason I have done it [vote] is through my parents – they have always voted and I've grown up seeing them vote. But a lot of my friends don't. Simply because it's not fashionable, it doesn't seem to be made a big thing. It's not talked about greatly. (Sarah, aged 23)

The official turnout figure for the 1997 General Election was 71.6% of the electorate, the lowest post-Second World War number (Heath and Taylor, 1999:166). The extremely low turnouts in subsequent by-elections in Kensington (29.8%), Wigan (25%) and Leeds Central (19.6%, also a postwar record low), are a further indication of the declining relevance of the democratic institutions in the eyes of the nation's citizens. There is a strong popular feeling that 'politicians' are not an appropriate authority for rationing or prioritising health and welfare; their democratic mandate does not seem to confer legitimacy on them. However, there is no popular consensus on an alternative legitimate expression of collective sentiment. As Sally Greengross of Age Concern said at the final Millennium Debate of the Age (Islington, 6 December 1999), 'There is general agreement that health service resources should be rationed in an open and transparent way, but no agreement about who should do it and the criteria to be used'.

Increasing numbers of people lack confidence in the political system's ability to deliver social benefits and social reform. This sentiment is felt more strongly in some places and some age groups than in others, but it was a clear theme of discussions on the role of politics in our focus groups. People are even pessimistic about the future of the Health Service despite that fact that it is an extremely popular institution. Following an opinion poll for the Millennium Debate of the Age in Devon, it was possible for Exeter Age Concern to summarise the attitudes to the National Health Service, in a predominantly conservative county that also contains a high proportion of elderly people, in the following terms:

> The strong feeling coming through the survey is of the importance people attach to the National Health Service and the sentiments of affection and concern that people have for it. There is strong attachment to the founding principles of a free service available at the point of need. People are aware of and have views about current Health Service issues such as rationing of healthcare, proper resourcing for the NHS, and care for frail elderly people. They would like it run in a way that both prevents ill-health and offers status and dignity to staff and older people. They want the service to be comprehensive and free but there are doubts and anxieties about whether this will be sustained. The sense of community and pride in the Health Service becomes translated into concerns about those seen to threaten or undermine the institution, be these incompetent or inefficient managers, self-seeking politicians, or the undeserving. Devon people are a diverse population with many ideas and opinions, the vast majority would wish to see a welfare state providing for the health and welfare of older people through the next century. (Age Concern Exeter, 1999)

Yet despite the highest esteem and value accorded to the NHS, two-thirds of Devonians disagreed with the statement 'The Health Service will be in better shape in 30 years' time than it is now.' There is a profound pessimism about the willingness and ability of the welfare state to deliver in the future, even though people believe in its principles and express a willingness to pay increased taxes to support it. The fact that there are large numbers of voters in the older age groups shows no signs of conveying greater power on them – pensioner power is not causing political instability; rather, it is the unwillingness of successive governments to meet the strong public expectations for the state to fulfil its duties towards older people that constitutes a crisis of legitimacy.

Generations and Political Attitudes

Is there is a negative effect of demographic change, stemming not from greater numbers of older voters, but from fewer young voters? It could be speculated that the relatively small number of younger voters and their tendency not to vote result in a lack of competition between parties to inspire and recruit this generation. Youth unemployment and the 'poll tax' among other factors made young people very anti-Tory during the 1990s. It would have been extremely difficult for the Conservatives to devise initiatives that would appeal to them.

Mannheim (1927) argued that generation replacement is necessary for social dynamism. His analysis of generations using historical evidence from mid-nineteenth-century Germany suggests that the impact of new ideas and aspirations is mediated through social movements and in particular crystallised and made effective by a younger generation's struggles to replace the previous, established generation of power holders. If it cannot be shown that the increasing numbers of older voters have a direct effect on the attitudes and behaviour of political parties and their leaders and strategists, is it possible that there are indirect effects of such demographic change? It has been suggested that there are positive benefits to society from the 'circulation' of generations, the circulation of elites, and the dynamic impact that this cycle of replacement has on social life. Older people, it has been argued, are small 'c' conservative. Hence politics involving a greater number of older participants and/or a lesser number of younger ones becomes small 'c' conservative. That is to say that it exhibits little desire for change, is characterised by appeals to past glories, and articulates no new vision of the future. This would reflect Mannheim's dystopian image of a society without a circulation of generations.

However, the view that older people are 'naturally' conservative needs to be critically examined and may merely be yet another negative stereotype of older people. This argument also depends on the view that political ideas and values are subject to exploration and examination in early adulthood but then become largely fixed for the rest of adult life (Jennings and Niemi, 1981). If there were a slowing of the circulation of elites, if the upcoming generation were inhibited from taking leadership

positions by the numerical superiority of the preceding generation, then one
would expect conservative politics to dominate.

It might be possible to argue that the increasing proportion of older
people in the Western demographic profile is responsible for the centre-
right orientation of politics and 'family values' and 'moral majority' social
policies in the 1980s and 1990s. This is an argument based on the cultural
assumption that older people are conservative with a small 'c'. What is the
evidence of a small 'c' conservative political agenda? It is important in this
instance to distinguish social conservatism from right-wing politics and
social and economic policies. 'New Right' economic and social policies
have been characterised as radical and a driving force for social change.
However, this trend to social conservatism may be seen in 'law and order'
issues. Crime is an issue that older people feel is particularly salient.

> We like the idea of the reassuring Bobby on the Beat, and community
> policing is something that we strongly endorse, and we've seen how
> Labour talked about increasing police resources before the General
> Election, and there are now far fewer police than there were beforehand,
> and we think that older people, obviously, tend to be much more in fear of
> crime. Whether they are any more victims of crime or not, I'm not sure,
> actually, but certainly they are more concerned about it. And I think they
> would be more reassured if they saw a more visible police presence.
> (Christopher Rennard, Liberal Democrat, OPPOL interview)

Crime is both an age and a generation issue. It is an age issue
because people who are older feel themselves to be frailer and therefore
more vulnerable to violence. Further, the old are seen as victims, while the
perpetrators are seen as young. The generational dimension comes from the
collective memory of a time when there was much less crime and more
community solidarity. Older people refer to the days when front doors were
left open, and you could trust neighbours and tradesmen, and remark that
'our generation' have had to *learn* to distrust others.

Another issue that is potentially significant to older votes is that of
trade unions. Anti-union sentiment was a vote winner for the Tories in the
1980s. However, it was suggested that:

> ...[The] general secretary of the TUC – has been elevated into ogre of the
> week. Only John Major can save the country from a trade union-
> dominated Blair government. Remember the bad old days when Jack
> Jones and Hugh Scanlon were invited to tea at 10 Downing Street? The
> answer to that question is: not unless you are over 40. But Michael
> Heseltine – brilliant originator of the ventriloquist dummy poster ... will
> do his best to remind you. His problem is that Jack Jones is now the
> lovable octogenarian champion of the old age pensioners, and Hugh

Scanlon is a member of the House of Lords. (*Guardian*, 21 April 1997, 'Tories call up old ogres', Roy Hattersley)

Politics has moved on. Trade union power was greatly undermined by the politics of Thatcherism and by the economic changes that saw the British economy retreat from large-scale industrial production. New Labour has assiduously distanced itself from the trade union movement. What is interesting in the context of our question (Are older people becoming more politically powerful?), is that the demon of the trade unions is not recreated as a threat from militant pensioners but has become rather the 'loveable octogenarian champion'.

Another generationally important issue is Europe, which played a role in the 1997 election and appears likely to play an even bigger role in 2001. Polls suggest that older people are more nationalistic than are younger people, who tend to be more cosmopolitan in their attitudes:

> Younger people have a very low turnout rate. Older people tend to be much more Eurosceptic, and hostile to the European Union, and therefore our campaigns tend to centre very much on arguments about saving the pound versus European Monetary Union. With older people turning out, that accounts partly for why the Conservatives appeared to do so well. (Christopher Rennard, Liberal Democrats, OPPOL interview)

This sentiment is demonstrated in data collected by the EU itself in its Eurobarometer survey (1996), which are shown in Charts 9.1 and 9.2. They demonstrate how anti-EU sentiment and identification with the nation (rather then Europe or region) are age-related. Europe is an important issue to the Conservatives and one in which their divisions proved a major weakness in the 1997 General Election. However, it was less important to the public. In contrast to Europe, domestic issues are seen as important by the general public. Reporting on John Major campaigning in Leeds, the *Times* stated:

> Wavering Leeds Tories referred to the state of the NHS, schools and job worries. Europe, the issue that has bedevilled Major's government for the past four years, was low in their priorities. (*Times*, 27 April 1997, 'In the Gutter' feature, Grice et al.)

Older people are generally more Eurosceptic than the younger age groups, but this has a generational rather than an age basis. We may

Chart 9.1 Percentage by age group who consider membership of the EU a bad thing

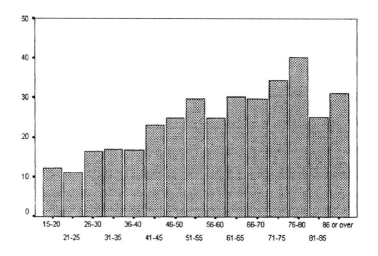

Source: Authors' analysis of Eurobarometer, January - March 1996.

surmise that this is due to a patriotism shared by people who have lived through the war, but whatever the case, this is an issue that older people do and will have a say about. Interviews with politicians like Peter Bottomley indicate they are very aware of this: 'The Europe issue looks as though it's going to stop people feeling British and that will play a big part, and especially with the elderly.' Party strategists also show concern that Europe is a strong issue for older people.

> The one issue which again is strongly differentiated [by age] and which may be coming more to the fore is Europe. Older people are a lot more sceptical about Europe and the Euro than are younger people and that clearly is a big factor. (Party campaign organiser, OPPOL interview)

However, there is evidence that older people, as a group, share opinions on specific issues they feel have significant national importance,

Chart 9.2 Percentage by age group who identify with nation rather than Europe or region

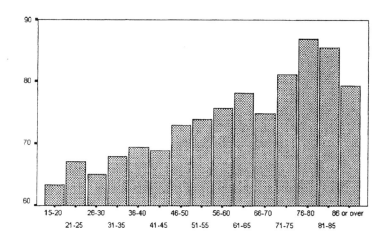

Source: Authors' analysis of Eurobarometer, January - March 1996.

which may sway the way they intend to vote in the future. These issues can better be described as 'generational' rather than as 'age group' issues (Park, 2000; Vincent et al., 2001). The two most important aspects of generational issues are that they are conceived of as having national importance (relating to the good of the country rather than the good of a minority) and that they are views shared by a generation of people because of their common experience and knowledge.

> The elderly are involved in particular [Conservative] associations. In the ... association many of their active members are elderly so they are involved but they aren't there for selfish reasons. They are there for national reasons or local community reasons. (Peter Bottomley, Conservative Party MP, OPPOL interview)

It is true that an ageing population potentially provides older people with sufficient strength to influence election outcomes. Nevertheless, there is much evidence to suggest that older people will not mobilise to use this strength to further their own self-interests. However, where older people share opinions regarding issues of national importance (which as a generation with shared experiences they are likely to do) their influence may be substantial.

> The fact is that older people are increasingly the key element in the electorate. Government and the political parties generally are on fragile ground if they think that that key voting strength will not become polarised and exploited at some stage. It isn't happening now, although quite clearly the disenchantment with the government seems to be increasing with older people (that's what MORI tells us). If that is so, that is already beginning to demonstrate a polarisation amongst older people. What is not happening at the moment, and we are not the people to do it, is that, their [voting strength] is not being exploited. Now, I think a clever politician is going to start to recognise that and is going to start talking the right words, to really begin to polarise that voting strength and use it tactically and strategically. (Michael Lake, Director of Help the Aged, OPPOL interview)

Conclusion

The direction of the New Labour government suggests that citizens' rights in a welfare state have a limited future as a route to accessing healthcare and welfare provision. The lack of effectiveness of pensioner power expressed through the political system suggests that this tide is unlikely to be stemmed. The danger in the future is the existence, alongside a number of affluent pensioners, of an underclass of older people with fragmented work histories surviving on a basic minimum of stigmatised welfare handouts. An agenda that stresses the duty to work and emphasises the creation of a welfare system in which 'work pays' undervalues the social contribution of non-employed people – including those who have retired. There will be further problems that will unfold from this approach to welfare if, in the future, the state cannot guarantee opportunities for employment and thus the rewards from work. This will mean that large numbers of the upcoming generations of older people will fall into the underclass.

Consumer power also has severe limitations as a route to health and welfare provision (cf. Warde, 1994). Not only are there the inherent insecurities of market fluctuations, as indicated by the current low returns of annuity-based financial instruments, but other power structures also constrain the consumer clout of older people. The effectiveness of consumer citizenship for individual older people depends to a great extent on the resources and deficits, both in finance and in health, that they accumulate over a lifetime. Reliance on capitalist markets then generates huge risks that the individual cannot fully anticipate or cover themselves against.

The 'Third Way', Blair's reform of welfare, is no radical solution to the current crisis of the welfare state. In practice it means a reduction of the welfare state to a minimum means-tested safety net, and providing the framework and encouragement for individual savings and provision. Securing the future health and welfare of any population is necessarily an insurance process – individual savings cannot substitute for collective protection against these risks. In different parts of the world, usually depending on their specific history, people see private insurance companies or the state as the more reliable instruments for pooling risk.

Higgs (1997) argues that it is not accidental that active seniors purposely separate themselves from means-tested and needs-assessed rights of social citizenship to welfare provision while championing citizen access to health and pensions. He suggests that this is why acute healthcare is very much a political issue in the UK and long-term institutional and community care is not. It appears that the battle for citizen access to long-term residential care has been lost, and the battle for hearts and minds over the welfare state is almost lost. It is not that the National Health Service is not seen as highly desirable, but rather that younger people have been increasingly convinced that it is unsustainable.

Conclusion

Older People and Politics

Bornat (1998) points out that, historically speaking, pensioners have not voted according to age-related issues. It was expected in the 1992 General Election that Conservative pensioners would change their votes to Labour in the light of the 'Conservatives ending the link between pension and earnings, freezing the Christmas bonus and breaking the consensus in relation to health and social care' (Bornat, 1998:194). Yet this was not the case. The evidence from this study indicates that older people, like the rest of the population, do not vote on single issues or specifically age-related issues alone. The pensioners' movement's persistent attempts to mobilise older people around the single issue of restoring the link between pensions and earnings has had relatively little impact.

Is it not possible to mobilise older people around age-group issues if they do not identify themselves as a group. Such mobilisation requires people to think of themselves as part of a group and therefore identify with common issues. Defining the category 'older people' is itself highly problematic. Chronological age is a continuum; it does not automatically segment people into particular age groups. Older people are a varied group with widely different backgrounds, involved in a variety of activities that often have little or nothing to do with age. Few people want to consider themselves as old; many older people strongly feel that age should be socially and politically irrelevant. There is a reluctance amongst older people to define themselves as old, and it is possible that this prevents them from identifying with age-group issues.

> I think it's fair to say that it's probably a generation that doesn't identify with issues of older people. They don't consider themselves old. Old is still stereotypically the pretty frail, probably female, probably fairly poor, over 80-something and that's not what people want to join. (Mervyn Kohler, Help the Aged, OPPOL interview)

If older people do not identify themselves as a group with specific needs and desires and are not willing to vote on age-related issues, it is unlikely that an ageing population will influence election outcomes in their favour. Ginn and Arber state that 'the claim that older people have used, or will use, their growing numerical power in elections to further their own interests at the expense of younger people is misconceived' (1999:164). Midwinter (1992:282) goes even further by saying that he cannot see any chance for the success of the pensioners' movement in the foreseeable future.

Challenges for the Pensioners' Movement

Three key problems for the political effectiveness of the pensioners' movement emerge: the diversity of interests with a stake in the pensions issue, the problems of organising older people on a national basis, and cultural issues about old age and its identification as an appropriate basis for political solidarity. The important areas of social difference that can inhibit older people in achieving political cohesion include class, age, gender, ethnicity, benefit status, savings and health. Two cultural aspects to the effectiveness of the pensioners' movement also emerge as particularly important: the cultural evaluation of old age itself and the political culture of the UK.

Diversity

Is there sufficient common interest among older people for them to sustain a coherent and effective political movement? Older people are as diverse a set of people as is the general public as a whole. This is reflected in the wide range of interest groups and organisations involved in the pensioners' movement. The roots of the movement traditionally aligned older people with organisations that have an interest in social welfare. The state pension itself was the result of a campaign that brought together a broad alliance of church, charitable foundations, self-help societies, voluntary organisations, the co-operative movement and the Trade Union Congress as well as allies in the Liberal and Labour parties. The current movement is neither a coherent 'single issue' pressure group, nor a ragbag of pensioners' groups. It is a movement that reflects its heterogeneous membership, and the diverse and constantly evolving support it receives from the wider community. Is it possible to set clear objectives and sustain a powerful campaign that will carry force and conviction in the face of such diversity? It would appear that the future of the NPC, which remains the most unifying force within the movement, depends on how it resolves this situation.

Employment history and class One way of looking at pensions is as deferred wages. Thus the structure of employment in different occupations and in particular patterns of remuneration, job security and collective bargaining has an important effect on how income in retirement is viewed. Occupational history is then important to attitudes to the state-provided scheme for retirement income. Occupational elites, such as civil servants, the military and the police, who have a single large stable employer (in these examples, the state), have been in comparative terms well provided for in old age. Those in manual work, with short-term or casual contracts and who work in trades characterised by a multiplicity of small employers such as dockers, building workers and shop workers, do less well from occupational-based schemes. Thus, within the trade union movement it was the large general manual workers' unions, such as the Transport and General Workers, NUPE (public sector manual workers now part of UNISON), and the General and Municipal Workers Union, who provided leadership and were most keen to support the pensioners' movement. Those with strong occupational pension schemes, like miners (NUM) and railwaymen (NUR) did not feel the same pressures. The changing employment structure in the last quarter of the twentieth century, with fewer manual workers, fewer craft skills in heavy industry, less stability of employment and a multiplicity of public, private and occupational pensions, will diversify people's interest in the state pension still further. Conflicts from the past over the relationship between trade unions and the pensioners' organisations may be of less salience in the future. The increasing complexity of the labour market will result in diverse interests in old age and thus the ability to create a solid campaigning organisation with a sharp focus on the state pension. The decline of class politics has been widely debated (see for example Harvey, 1989; Waters, 1997) and undermines the power of appeal to the common interest of working people to protect the value of the pension. On the other hand, appeals to common age-based interests have not yet emerged as an alternative basis of solidarity and collective action.

Older versus younger pensioners   Older pensioners, particularly women, are less likely to benefit from occupational pensions. Pensioners of different ages are also differently affected by the mix of savings, benefits and pensions that reflects the changing circumstances of different cohorts. The oldest pensioners tend to be the poorest, even though some benefits are restricted to the oldest age groups and some of the factors that deprived the very old of successive improvements in National Insurance benefits have ceased to have effect. Older pensioners whose savings have run down find themselves in a complex and confusing situation of eligibility for some benefits and not for others. The most onerous of these is residential care, which has been removed as an NHS, and thus free, provision. Many writers make the distinction between the Third Age and the Fourth Age, the Third

Age being a time of leisure, personal growth and achievement post-retirement, while the Fourth Age is a period of physical limitation and incapacity prior to death. The balance of priorities between pensions and disposable income on the one hand, and health and social care provision on the other varies between different groups of older people. There is not necessarily solidarity amongst older people based on benefit status or sickness. Indeed, most older people reject these stigmatised statuses and do not want to be labelled as welfare recipients or as sick.

Gender Most older people are women and they play a significant part in the pensioners' movement, but considering their numbers they are not as visible as might be expected. There are of course many powerful, articulate women in the pensioners' movement – to mention Barbara Castle, Teresa Le Fort (Chair of the Greater London Forum for the Elderly), and Dorothy Rhodes (Chair of the National Federation of Old Age Pensions Associations) is to illustrate the point rather than single them out or suggest they are generating a specifically older women's agenda. Yet that older women's agenda exists:

> Rights of older women: In Europe the vast majority of the elderly population are women and they have a positive contribution to make to society through their knowledge, experience, creativity and skills. They are a valuable resource that often is unacknowledged. And indeed, the reality of their lives in today's ageist and sexist society is that many are single, alone and living below the poverty line, especially in the more vulnerable higher age groups. (Opening part of a statement adopted at the 12th International Congress of the European Federation for the Welfare of the Elderly, May 1988, reprinted in Bernard and Meade, 1993:194-6)

Bornat (1998) suggests that pensioners' organisations may not give full weight to issues of gender. The relative discrimination against women in old age has been documented by, amongst others, Arber and Ginn (1991, 1995); and Bernard and her colleagues (1993, 2000) have raised awareness within the academic community of women's distinctive experience of being old.

Ethnicity Different ethnic minorities have different kinds of interests in old age. These differences can stem from different histories of migration, different experiences of employment, cultural differences in family and household, and experiences of racism and exclusion. For example, Jewish and Polish communities have much higher proportions of older people than do the Bangladeshi or Nigerian communities. Language, diet and religion can be vital to aspects of health and social care for minority elders. The contrasting experiences of minority women as independent earners and heads of households have profound impacts on pensions and benefits. These concerns can be articulated at the local level through, for example, forums and community organisations. It is more difficult for this diversity to be reflected in national arenas.

Those on means-tested benefits The pensioners' movement needs to develop a greater sophistication in dealing with the diversity and complexity of older people's financial circumstances. There is an increasing amount of pensioner poverty: the number of pensioners in England with incomes below half the national average income has increased from 1.2 million in 1979 to 2.4 million twenty years later (Peter Townsend, *Guardian*, 11 May 2000). At the same time, in recent years occupational pensions have raised many pensioners well beyond a minimum standard of living. This divergence of wealth and income presents a political dilemma for the traditional pensioners' movement. Those who are campaigning for the basic state pension to be uprated have to take into account the fact that, however symbolically important the basic pension is, there are many older people for whom this priority has no immediate financial benefit. There are a set of means-tested benefits that raise the basic pension to what is currently called by government the Minimum Income Guarantee. Poor pensioners represent 40% of the 4.7 million people claiming Housing Benefit. Merely raising the basic pension does not help these people, as it merely decreases their means-tested benefits; unless, that is, the pension is raised by a very substantial amount – in the order of £10 per week for a single person. The campaign materials of the pensioners' movement tend not to acknowledge the way in which raising the basic pension would affect benefits:

> Poor pensioners on means-tested benefits will see their income support benefit reduced pound per pound by any increase in basic pension receipt. Paradoxically, most of the gains will go to better-off pensioners not on means-tested benefits, who will enjoy the full increase in their basic pension. (Stears, 1998:13)

The pensioners' organisations have campaigned vigorously on the consequences of detaching the relationship between the pension and average earnings. They present data that demonstrates how much pensioners have lost by this move (see Chart 7.1). However, whatever the merits of a National Insurance-based system with a basic state pension linked to earnings, these figures do not translate directly into older people's household budgets. Not only does the complexity of pension schemes potentially divide older people, but the complexity and structure of means-tested benefits give them different short-term financial interests. The importance of Housing Benefit to older individuals varies in importance according to tenure and the significant regional variations in housing costs. A number of informed interviewees suggested to us that this was a key factor in the absence of a mass movement around the subject of pensions. The pensioners' movement is confronted by successive governments that seem determined to pursue a means-testing policy on income support in old age. The movement as a whole has to find ways to debate and reconcile short- and long-term objectives – more income in the pockets of the older poor now, and a decent pension for all senior citizens as a permanent feature of the welfare state.

The 'nearly poor' with small savings There is another group of pensioners who feel particularly cheated by the current system. These are people who have made savings for their old age and who, by virtue of those savings, lose eligibility for means-tested supplementary pension and other benefits. The expansion of means-tested benefits to provide income support for poorer older people has led to a poverty trap. Many older people are indignant that they worked and saved all their lives and are now effectively penalised for their prudence. They are excluded, as they see it, from means-tested benefits paid to those whom they characterise as less diligent and more feckless. In practice a significant number of pensioners fail to claim means-tested benefits to which they are entitled. Many groups have campaigned on this issue and the government has conducted a series of studies on benefit take-up (Costingan et al., 2000). It is this group who would most directly benefit from a substantial increase in the basic state pension.

Existing v. future pensioners There are those who criticise the pensioners' movement for concentrating on those currently in receipt of the state pension. Arguably those most disadvantaged by pension 'reform' in the 1980s and 1990s have been those yet to receive their pension. From this perspective there are a range of alliances that need to be strengthened if the pensioners' movement is to become more influential. Younger sections of the population need to be convinced that they have common interests with today's older people. Such issues as the level of the current pension do not offer much in the way of an incentive for younger people to move closer to the movement. The leadership itself shows an overriding concern for 'today's pensioners':

> ...the NPC is not so much concerned with the future, although I think it is important to be concerned about it because of our children and grandchildren; we are concerned about the present-day pensioners. This is why I prefer the idea of negotiating, to get in the minds of ministers. We

are talking about the present, about those who have contributed to the NI fund, in a sense those who have made all the sacrifices. (Jack Jones, President of the NPC, OPPOL interview)

While it is important to recognise current injustices, perhaps the key for the pensioners' movement's acquisition of political muscle is to rebuild links with future pensioners. Age Concern's (1999) Millennium Paper, 'Values and Attitudes in an Ageing Society', debates the impact of population ageing on democracy. While the authors are wrong, as we believe the evidence in this book shows, to talk about older people as being a powerful political force, they are right to advocate measures to foster a sense of community among all age groups. They suggest specific action to increase the awareness, for example through education, of all sections of society about the concerns and interests of generations other than their own. Sympathetic understanding is one thing; common interest is another. Increasing solidarity and avoiding conflict between generations require a proper identification of the real opponents of secure, well-funded state pensions for all.

Getting Organised

Older people's organisations share problems with other radical and campaigning organisations, but they also have their own specific problems. Organisations of older people appear to be divided into a multiplicity of groups that do not cooperate easily. Older people are a diverse population, and these various differences are mirrored in a diversity of organisations. Age also brings with it a personal history of both commitment and enmity. The older you are, the more past loyalties and past disagreements can complicate decision making over priorities and campaigning strategies in the present. This problem of fragmentation is also reflected in the local and regional bases of many of the organisations. There seem to be distinct problems of mobilisation and coordination on a national level. Pensioners' Voice allows its local branches to decide policy by means of a tortuous process of grassroots democracy, which takes place at its conference only once a year.

> The way the policy of the Federation is made, historically, has always been from local people in local branches. It is conference which decides policy, not the executive, so local people in local branches submit motions.[39] They are vetted by the Standing Orders Committee. They come

---

[39] A recent (1999) motion, presented at the annual conference, was to instruct the National Executive Committee 'to urge H.M. Government to reverse the trend of penalising thrift, by rewarding those who have tried to help themselves through sacrifices in their

to conference, are presented by delegates, seconded usually with a great deal of discussion and a great deal of to-ing and fro-ing. There is often a lot of opposition but they are voted on, and providing they get the appropriate majority of votes, they are then taken to the Executive. Which means, after conference, they are then absorbed into policy and taken to Parliament to MPs – so this has been our direct line, from the person in the branch through to Parliament. (Conference Delegate, Llandudno 1999, OPPOL interview)

Organisations of older people have particular problems with continuity. The shelf life of the leadership and the cadres of activists is naturally shorter for older people than it is for other groups. Youth wings of political parties, as well as student organisations, have a similar problem as one cohort of leaders after another surpasses the age range of the organisation. While many older people are fit and healthy and not all are poor, as a social group they are less well-off, have greater difficulties with mobility and are less well-educated than younger age groups are. This is reflected in their preference for the parochial, face-to-face, community organisation rather than the more politically effective media-oriented national organisation. Both practical difficulties and the orientation and culture of older people may play a part in this pattern.

Cultural Problems

The dominant culture in Western democracies creates problems for the organisation of older people. Old age is so devalued and youthfulness such an ideal in terms of beauty, the arts, sciences and desirable personal qualities that no one wants to be old. It is difficult to create a positive identity for old age as a symbol that people wish to internalise and to which they wish to commit themselves (Biggs, 1997). People are more likely to organise around issues than around age groups or generations. Pensions and rights in the welfare state, around which most older people's organisations campaign, are seen by their members as universal rights, not ones specific to old age or to themselves.

The political culture and constitution of the UK structure political life in ways that affect older peoples' representation. The British 'first past the post' electoral system encourages the dominance of two-party politics. Further, in the British political tradition this has been thought of as left and right, that is, as an ideological or class divide. There is thus no tradition of sectional interests such as age groups or occupations seeking their own representation; neither is there a multiplicity of potentially electable parties

working lives, by increasing their spending power with a substantial increase in the State Pension' (Motion 4, passed unanimously).

amongst whom voters can pick and choose. In the second half of the twentieth century there has been a growth in single-issue pressure groups, who see their role as influencing existing parties and governments rather than participating in government. An older persons' party is unlikely to meet with success on the electoral battleground. In terms of a single-interest pressure group, the only viable option as an issue around which older people can unite is the value of the state pension. However, as indicated above, interests over the pension are fragmented and divide pensioners from pension contributors, and state pensioners from occupational or private pensioners.

These cultural factors combine in various ways. In terms of leadership, there are few nationally recognised leaders who want to transfer from their current political parties or organisations into older people's organisations. Further, the British political tradition and the devaluing of old age combine to limit the value of this career move for an aspiring leader looking for power and influence. The devaluation of old age makes it more difficult for older people's organisations to form effective coalitions and alliances. Access to the media to convey their message is restricted and distorted by negative images of old age. Some images are more media-friendly than others: pictures of furry animals, dolphins or children are more likely than pictures of older people to generate coverage and sympathy.

Strategic Alliances: Public Compassion v. Militant Self-help

Dilemmas over priorities and alliances are not new; they have always existed and were debated throughout the development of the pensioners' movement. Every development of the pension system has required a balance to be struck. Universalism and equity, on the one hand, has to be matched with financial constraints and the level of contributions and taxation on the other. Targeting resources at the most needy has to be balanced against the disincentive to save that means tests create. This balance is a political act that gives priority to some groups over others. However, motives other than self-interest form part of the equation and of people's understanding of the politics of old age.

The universality of the state pension gives all older people a common interest and makes it a logical central issue for the pensioners' movement. However, the diversity of the levels and sources of older people's incomes means that the impact of the state pension on their household budgets is in many cases not a strong motivation in terms of self-interest.

> I am not sure that people at home doing their household calculations are quite as persuaded by the economics of it. They are quite persuaded by the way it reflects a sense of moral injustice and a sense of being left behind ... and not having got what was deserved. (OPPOL interview with an informed London-based advocate on behalf of older people)

The financial resources and technical expertise of the major charities enable them to master and argue the specifics of benefits, pensions and allowances. Such expertise does not promote the solidarity engendered by the pensioners' organisations, who use the potent symbol of the national state pension – the community's recognition of a lifetime contribution to society – to stand for 'senior citizenship'. If there is a crisis of old-age politics, it is the reflection of a wider crisis in the relationship, the rights and duties owed, between the state and its citizens.

> It should be manifestly clear that it is an injustice in a society like ours to expect older people who've paid taxes and all the rest to live on the pittance that is handed out. (Bruce Kent, 70 years old, OPPOL interview)

The question can be asked: What is the moral basis for the claim to an income in old age? This claim is widely upheld as a statement in principle; the general public believe that older people should be supported financially in old age (see Table 8.3). The moral basis of this claim has to be expressed symbolically in order for a campaign to be effective. The effects will be very different depending on whether the claim is made as the self-proclaimed right of a citizen or on behalf of a deserving object of charity.

Are Older People Becoming More Powerful?

It is a natural reaction to believe that if there are more older people, then they should be more politically powerful. The naturalness of this belief comes from the normative framework that forms the ideological underpinning of a democratic society. This normative framework holds that all citizens are equal, and their votes all count equally. Therefore the majority wins elections and the political system expresses the will of the majority. Hence within this logic a greater number of older people means more votes and thus more power.

However, crucially, it depends on 'old age' offering a meaningful identity within which people act politically, for example, in how they cast their votes. Thus if people do not feel that age is an appropriate basis for political solidarity or action, then the changing proportions of age groups will not come to be reflected in the political process. It may be argued that older people acquire more power even if they are not conscious of age as a political factor. This would be plausible if other political actors believed that they were powerful and mediated their own actions in accordance with that belief. It might also be argued that age-related factors influence opinions on issues, parties, leaders and other factors that affect how people vote. In this way the political process is influenced indirectly, as those age-mediated opinions set political agendas and influence political mobilisation and the balance of power.

Older people do not by and large see themselves as powerful and tend to reject age as the basis for political action. Older voters justify their political actions in terms of an ideology of the greater good, looking after society as whole rather than a particular age group. However, the whole population, including older people, holds to the values of the welfare state. There is a widespread belief in older people as the deserving poor, or at least that people should not be neglected by the nation in their old age. Thus while there is greater debate and talk of the grey lobby influencing government, and people are asserting that the grey vote could swing the next election, this is unlikely to be the case. Much more significant are the images the major parties portray in terms of their policies and perceived willingness to look after older people. For the Labour Party the task is to reassure its core vote, indeed even to re-establish with them a sense that it is the natural party for social welfare and the care of the elderly. Motivating its core electorate to come out and vote was a key electoral problem for Labour in 1999 and 2000. For the Conservatives the task is to overcome the uncaring image of untrustworthy money-men that was the legacy of many years of government with Thatcherite policies. They too have to reassure the electorate that their plans for government will conform with the requisites of 'compassionate ageism'. Thus it is not the grey vote *per se* – self-aware older people voting for their own direct interest – that is significant; rather it is the way that the general electorate (including older people) perceives the welfare state.

Alan Walker has discussed what he calls a 'new politics of old age'. His argument, based on a Europe-wide view of older people's politics, points to increased activity by pensioners as a sign that they are becoming more important. In particular he regards the growth of forums and other evidence of increased local articulation of older people's views with optimism. Other optimists point to the social characteristics of the upcoming generation of older people and, particularly if they are in the age group themselves, point out the radical traditions and libertarian attitudes of those socialised in the 1960s. On the evidence of our research, the barriers, problems and limitations of older people's politics that we have found are likely to be repeated for future generations. Forums are important, but they do not amount to a cohesive political force. Many with a conscious identification with the sixties generation adamantly refuse to be thought of in terms of age – they 'hope they die before they get old'.[40]

Conclusion

It is difficult to find at the close of the twentieth century any evidence of a growth in the political strength of the older age groups. Evidence for an apparent lack of influence of older people, on the other hand, is twofold, first, in the character and activities of older people's organisations and, second, in the low priority given by party political elites to older voters. It is not possible to identify changes in the age profiles of party leaders that suggest that older people have become more desirable or effective as leaders of the nation. Further, there is little evidence of increased responsiveness by governments or political parties to organised groups of older people. It is difficult to find examples of political parties having been particularly enthusiastic or efficient in the identification of issues that are important to older voters, or having been sensitive to presenting issues in a manner that appeals to older people.

The pensioners' movement does not see itself as girding up for intergenerational conflict. On the contrary, a society in which age is less salient, particularly in determining access to work, wealth and welfare, is seen as both desirable and feasible. The fewer younger people in our society do not seem to become more valued because of their relative scarcity, and they have ceased to participate in the conventional political process in large numbers. The old and young do not get enough opportunities to work and the middle-aged work too much. If this ageism in the organisation of work and the distribution of its benefits can be redressed, then simplistic formulations of growing dependency ratios as a demographic timebomb will prove to be groundless.

The pensioners' movement is more than just the heroic last stand of class warriors. The courage, commitment and ideals that motivated people such as Jack Jones and Bill Goodwin, who were both members of the International Brigades in the fight against fascism in 1930s Spain and are stalwarts of the pensioners' movement now, are of vital contemporary relevance. The principle struggle against poverty and for social justice in which they are engaged is a struggle against the irresponsibility of footloose international capital. Those who follow the imperatives required to obtain the maximum short-term profit for their capital in global markets

---

[40] For the uninitiated, the words allude to the lyrics of the 1965 song 'My Generation' by Pete Townshend of The Who.

carry no sense of community or of loyalty between generations. For them, social solidarity is not a social value, merely a risk calculation. The old compromise between capital and labour that characterised Europe in the postwar era has been lost. What is needed to achieve the pensioners' movement's highest ideals is a more equitable balance of capital and labour at the global level, a balance of power that will reestablish on a worldwide scale, a commitment to creating and sustaining a less poverty-stricken and more equitable world.

Such a global readjustment is the necessary precursor to a reasonable future for the growing numbers of older people in the world. The achievement of this objective will require the inspiration to international solidarity shown by the volunteers to the International Brigades of the 1930s. Thus this book has illustrated the stubborn determination of the British financial elite to dismantle the institution of the state pension and the limited ability of the current pensioners' movement to combat it. But the world needs the grandparental generation, its senior citizens, to take their traditional role as guardians of communal collective responsibility for the future of the community and for future generations. The long-term survival of the world's people requires basic social solidarity, some worldwide sense of community that motivates us all to take the longer view. This can be seen most clearly in terms of the environment, but the same is also true for social welfare. It is the development of such a feeling for international social solidarity that will secure the future for social welfare and pension provision. The politics of old age is not about the past, it is about the future.

Bibliography

Achenbaum, A. W. (1983), *Shades of Gray: Old Age, American Values and Federal Policies since 1920*, Boston: Little, Brown and Company.

Achenbaum, A. W. (1997), 'Elder power: A new myth for a new age,' plenary presentation, The British Society of Gerontology Conference, Elder Power in the 21st Century, Bristol, 19-21 September 1997.

Age Concern (1999), *Network* (Issue 5), 7 July.

Age Concern (1999), *Millennium Papers – Values and Attitudes in an Ageing Society*, London: Age Concern.

Age Concern Cymru (1999), *Debate of the Age – Agenda for Wales*, Cardiff: Age Concern Cymru, October.

Age Concern Exeter (1999), *Ageing and the Future of Health and Social Care*, Exeter: Age Concern Exeter.

Age Concern in the South West (1999), *Demographic Change: an Opportunity. Response to the Regional Economic Strategy of the South West of England Regional Development Agency*, September.

Alderman, G. (1978), *British Elections: Myth and Reality*, London: Batsford.

Arber, S. and J. Ginn (1991), *Gender and Later Life*, London: Sage.

Arber, S. and J. Ginn (eds) (1995), *Connecting Gender and Ageing*, Buckingham: Open University Press.

Association of British Insurers (1999), *Stakeholder Pensions: Drawing Together the Threads*, Internal Briefing, Memo99\m121099.doc.

Association of Retired People and Those over 50 (1998), website, www.arp.org.uk, 12 July.

Baars, J. (1991), 'The Challenge of Critical Gerontology: The Problem of Social Constitution,' *Journal of Aging Studies* 5(3): 219-43.

Barbalet, J. M. (1988), *Citizenship: Rights, Struggle and Class Inequality*, Milton Keynes: Open University Press.

Bauman, Z. (1992), *Mortality, Immortality and Other Life Strategies*, Cambridge: Polity Press.

Bauman, Z. (1998), *Work, Consumerism and the New Poor*, Buckingham: Open University Press.

Beck, U. (1992), *Risk Society: Towards a New Modernity*, translated by Mark Ritter, London: Sage Publications.

Beetham, D. and K. Boyle (1995), *Introducing Democracy*, Cambridge: Polity Press: UNESCO Publishing.

Benington, J. (1996), *Local Strategies and Initiatives for an Ageing Population*, Warwick: Local Government Centre, Warwick Business School.

Bernard, M. and K. Meade (eds) (1993), *Women Come of Age*, London: Edward Arnold.

Bernard, M., J. Phillips, L. Machin, and V. Harding Davies (eds) (2000), *Women Ageing: Changing Identities, Challenging Myths*, London: Routledge.

Better Government for Older People (1999), *Making It Happen: The report of the first year of the Better Government for Older People Programme 1998-1999*, Wolverhampton: BGOP.

Better Government for Older People (1999/2000), *Making in Happen, Briefing 2*, Wolverhampton: BGOP.

Beveridge, W. (1942), *Social Insurance and Allied Services*, London: HMSO.

Biggs, S. (1997), 'Choosing Not To Be Old? Mask, Bodies and Identity Management in Later Life', *Ageing and Society* 17: 553-70.

Binstock, R. H. (1994), 'Changing Criteria in Old-Age Programs: The Introduction of Economic Status and Need for Services', *The Gerontologist*, 34: 726-730.

Binstock, R. H. (1997), 'The 1996 Election : Older Voters and Implications for Polices on Ageing', *The Gerontologist*, 37: 15-17.

Binstock, R. H. and C. L. Day (1995), 'Aging and Politics', in (eds) Binstock, R. H. et al., *Handbook of Aging and the Social Sciences*, 4th edition, San Diego: Academic Press.

Blackburn, R. (1999), 'The new collectivism: pension reform, grey capitalism and complex socialism', *New Left Review* 233: 3-65.

Blaikie, A. (1990), 'The Emerging Political Power of the Elderly in Britain 1908-1948', *Ageing and Society* 10: 17-39.

Bornat, J. (1998), 'Pensioners Organise: Hearing the Voice of Older People', in (eds) Bernard, M. and J. Phillips, *The Social Policy of Old Age*, London: The Centre for Policy on Ageing, pp. 183-199.

BPTUAA, (1996), 'Was it Betrayal?', *British Pensioner*, (New Series) 24, Winter, pp. 1-2.

Cabinet Office (1998), press release, 29 October.

Carrigan, M. and I. Szmigin (2000), 'Advertising in an ageing society', *Ageing and Society* 20(2): 217-33.

Carter, M. (1999), 'Advertisers wake up to the nifty fifties', *Independent*, 26 October.

Centre for Policy on Ageing (1997-98), Annual Report.

Charities Commission, Reports, 1969, 1979, 1981, 1986 App. A (b).

Conservative Party (1955), *United for Peace and Progress: The Conservative and Unionist Party's Policy*, http://www.psr.keele.ac.uk/area/uk/man/con55.htm

Cook, Fay Lomax (1996), 'Can Public Support for Programs for Older Americans Survive?', http://www.library.nwu.edu/publications/nupr/cook.html, Center for Urban Affairs and Policy Research, Northwestern University.

Costingan, P., H. Finch, B. Jackson, R. Legard and J. Ritchie (2000), 'Overcoming Barriers: Older People and Income Support', DSS Research Report No. 100, London: HMSO.

Denver, D. (1994), *Elections and Voting Behaviour*, London: Harvester.

Denver, D. T. and G. Hands (1999), 'Constituency Campaigning in the 1997 General Election' (computer file), Colchester, Essex: The Data Archive (distributor), SN: 3922.

Department for Education and Employment (1999), 'Learning in Later Life', Report of Conference held in Wolverhampton, 3-4 February, PP51/38448/699/63, London: DfEE.

Department of Social Security (1997), 'Special Role for Jack Jones and NPC in Pensions Review', press release, 17 July.

Department of Social Security (1997), 'Swift and Substantial Progress in Pensions Review', press release, 24 September.

Department of Social Security (1997), press release, 97/192, 2 October.

Department of Social Security (1998), 'New Ambitions for our Country: A New Contract for Welfare' Green Paper: cm 3805, March.

Department of Social Security (1998), 'Building a Better Britain for Older People', consultation document produced for the ministerial group on old people, November.

Department of Social Security (1998), 'A New Contract for Welfare: Partnership in Pensions' Green Paper: cm 4179, 15 December.

Department of Social Security (1999), The Welfare Reform and Pensions Bill – Regulatory Impact Assessment, 2 August.

Dunleavy, P., A. Gamble, I. Holliday and G. Peele (eds) (1997), *Developments in British Politics*, Basingstoke: Macmillan.

Elias, N. (1996), *The Germans*, Oxford: Basil Blackwell.

Estes, C. L. (1979), *The Aging Enterprise*, San Francisco: Jossey-Bass.

Estes, C. L. (1989), 'Cost containment and the elderly: conflict or challenge?' *Journal of the American Geriatrics Society* 36(1): 68-72.

Estes, C. L., L. E. Gerard, J. Sprague Zones and J. H. Swan (1984b), *Political Economy, Health and Aging*, Boston: Little, Brown and Company.

Estes, C. L., K. Linkins and E. Binney (1996), 'The Political Economy of Aging', in (eds) R. Binstock and L. George, *Handbook of Aging and the Sciences*, New York: Academic Press, pp. 346-361.

Estes, C. L. and M. Minkler, (1984a), *Readings in the Political Economy of Aging*, Farmingdale, New York: Baywood.

Estes, C. L. and J. H. Swan (1993), *The Long-Term Care Crisis: Elders Trapped in the No-Care Zone*, Newbury Park, California: Sage.

Eurobarometer (1997), 'Mega-Survey: Policies and Practices' (computer file), Colchester, Essex: The Data Archive (distributor), 17 July, SN: 3755.

European Commission, (1996), *European Economy* (No. 3), Brussels: Directorate-General for Economic and Financial Affairs.

Evans, G. and P. Norris (eds) (1999), *Critical Elections*, London: Sage.

Falk, R. (1994), 'The Making of Global Citizenship', in (ed) Bart van Steenbergen *The Condition of Citizenship*, London: Sage, pp. 127-40.

Featherstone, M. and A. Wernick (1995), *Images of Ageing*, London: Routledge.

Field, F. (1999), Supplementary Memorandum Submitted by the Rt Hon Frank Field, MP (Cp 30a), Minutes of Evidence Taken before the Social Security Committee, Wednesday, 3 November.

Financial Times (1999) 'Minister says state pensioners will live in "poverty"', 21 October.

Frean, A. (1999), 'Spend, spend pensioners are new rich', *The Times*, Tuesday, 27 July.

Fulks, T. (1996), 'Geezer Rip-off: The older generation's greed is stifling the younger one, and Tom's mad', www.tomfulks.com, 20 May.

Giddens, A. (1982), 'Class Division, Class Conflict and Citizenship Rights', *Profiles and Critiques in Social Theory*, London: Macmillan.

Giddens, A. (2000), *The Third Way and its Critics*, Cambridge: Polity Press.

Gilleard, C. (1996), 'Consumption and Identity in Later Life: Toward a Cultural Gerontology', *Ageing and Society* 16: 489-498.

Gilleard, C. and P. Higgs (1998), 'The Social Limits of Old Age', conference paper, British Society of Gerontology Conference, 'Ageing: All Our Tomorrows', Sheffield, 18-20 September.

Ginn, J. and S. Arber (1999), 'The Politics of Old Age in the UK', in (eds) Walker, A. and G. Naegele, *The Politics of Old Age in Europe*, Buckingham: Open University Press, pp. 152-167.

Goodman, D. (1987), *No Thanks to Lloyd George: The forgotten story – how the pension was won*, Newcastle under Lyme, Staffordshire: D. Goodman.

Greater London Forum for the Elderly (1998/99), Annual Report.

Greater London Forum for the Elderly (1999), leaflet, May.

Greater London Forum for the Elderly (1999), Annual Report.

Greater London Forum for the Elderly (2000), *Senior London*, (Newsletter), April/May 2000.

Greater London Pensioners' Association (2000), *Review of the Greater London Authority Act*, London: GLPA.

Guardian (1999), 'Elderly "Neglected by NHS"' and 'Ageist Health Barriers', 8 November.

Guibernau, M. (1996), *Nationalisms*, London: Polity Press.

Haber, C. and B. Gratton (1994), *Old Age and the Search for Security: An American Social History*, Bloomington: Indiana University Press.

Harvey, D. (1989), *The Condition of Postmodernity: An Inquiry into the Origins of Cultural Change*, Oxford: Blackwell.

Hawkes, C. and A. Garman, (1995), *Perceptions of Non-State Pensions*, In-house Report No. 8, Social Research Branch, Department of Social Security.

Hay, C. (1999), *The Political Economy of New Labour: Labouring Under False Pretences?*, Manchester: Manchester University Press.

Hayden, C., A. Boaz and F. Taylor (1999), *Attitudes and Aspiration of Older People: A Qualitative Study*, DSS Research Report 102, London: HMSO.

Heath, A., R. Jowell, J. K. Curtice and P. Norris (1998), 'British General Election Survey 1997' (computer file), Colchester, Essex: The Data Archive (distributor), 2 July 1998, SN:3887.

Heath, A. and B. Taylor (1999), 'New Sources of Abstention?', in (eds) G. Evans and P. Norris, *Critical Elections: British Parties and Voters in Long-term Perspective*, London: Sage, pp. 164-180.

Held, D. (1995), *Democracy and the Global Order: From Modern State to Cosmopolitan Governance*, Stanford: Stanford University Press.

Help the Aged (1999) *Policy Update* (Edition 12), August.

Hibbs, J. (political correspondent) (1999), *Daily Telegraph*, p. 5, Tuesday, 28 September.

Higgs, P. (1995), 'Citizenship and Old Age: The End of the Road?', *Ageing and Society* 15: 535-550.

Higgs, P. (1997), 'Citizenship Theory and Old Age: From Social Rights to Surveillance', in (eds) A. Jamieson, S. Harper and C. Victor, *Critical Approaches to Ageing and Later Life*, Buckingham: Open University Press, pp. 118-31.

Hills, J. (1993), *The Future of Welfare*, York: Joseph Rowntree Trust.

Hills, J. (1996), 'Does Britain Have a Welfare Generation?', in (ed) A. Walker, *The New Generational Contract*, London: UCL Press, pp. 56-80.

House of Commons All Party Parliamentary Group for Pensioners (1992), Annual Report.

House of Lords (1990/1), Second Annual Report of the All Party Group on Ageing.

House of Lords (1994), Fifth Annual Report of the All Party Group on Ageing.

Hussey, J. (1999), '"An inheritance of fear": Older people and the workhouse in the twentieth century', paper presented to British Society of Gerontology Conference, Bournemouth, 17-19 September.

Isin, E. F. and P. K. Wood (1999), *Citizenship and Identity*, London: Sage.

Jackson, S. (1998), *Britain's Population*, London: Routledge.

Jennings, M. K. and R. G. Niemi (1981), *Generations and Politics: A Panel Study of Young Adults and Their Parents*, Princeton: Princeton University Press.

Johnson, P. (ed) (1994), *Twentieth century Britain: Economic, Social, and Cultural Change*, London: Longman.

Johnson, P. C. Conrad and D. Thomson (eds) (1989), *Workers versus Pensioners*, Manchester: Manchester University Press.

Johnson, P. and J. Falkingham (1992), *Ageing and Economic Welfare*, London: Sage.

Jones, N. (1997), *Campaign 1997: How the General Election was Won and Lost*, London: Indigo.

Joshi, H. (ed) (1989), *The Changing Population of Britain*, Oxford: Blackwell.

Katz, S. (1996), *Disciplining Old Age: The Formation of Gerontological Knowledge*, Charlottesville: University of Virginia Press.

Labour Party (1997), Manifesto.

Labour Research, Social Service News (1958), 'Plan for Poverty in Old Age', November, pp. 176-177.

Labour Research, Social Service News (1959), 'The Tenacity of Privilege', February, pp. 29-31.

Lewis, P. (1999), 'Pensioners seek new deal', *Daily Telegraph*, Saturday, 31 July.

Lynes, A. (2000), 'Another Pensions Scandal?' submission to the government on stakeholder pensions 1998-99, London: NPC.

Macnicol, J (1998), *The Politics of Retirement in Britain, 1878-1948*, Cambridge: Cambridge University Press.

Macnicol, J. and A. Blaikie (1989), 'The Politics of Retirement 1908-1948', in (ed) M. Jefferys, *Growing Old in the Twentieth Century*, London: Routledge.

Malthus, T. R. (1970[1798][1830]), *An essay on the principle of population; and, A summary view of the principle of population*, edited with an introduction by Antony Flew, Harmondsworth: Penguin.

Mann, M. (1987), 'Ruling Strategies and Citizenship', *Sociology* 21(3):339-354.

Mann, M. (1988), *War and Social Theory*, Oxford: Blackwell.

Mannheim, K. (1927), 'The Problem of Generations', reprinted in M. A. Hardy (ed) (1997), *Studying Aging and Social Change: Conceptual and Methodological Issues*, London: Sage.

Marshall, T. H. (1992), *Citizenship and Class*, London: Pluto.

Marwick, A. (1963), *The Explosion of British Society 1914-62*, London: Pan Books.

Midwinter, E. (1991), *The British Gas Report on Attitudes to Ageing*, British Gas (no place of publication given).

Midwinter, E. (1992), 'Old Age and Community Development', *Community Development Journal* 27(3):282.

Midwinter, E. and S. Tester (1987), *Polls Apart? Older Voters and the 1987 General Election*, London: Centre for Policy on Ageing.

Miles, J. (1990), *Towards Equality: How Pensions Campaigns are Changing – A Study of the Greater London Pensioners Association 1989-90*, MSc. thesis, King's College, University of London.

Miles, J. (1994), 'Slow Progress: Why a Political Framework is Necessary for the Evaluation of Pensioners' Campaigns', *Generations Review* 4 (1), 4-8.

Miller, D. (1995), 'Consumption as the Vanguard of History: A Polemic by way of Introduction', in (ed) D. Miller, *Acknowledging Consumption: A review of new studies*, London: Routledge, pp. 1-57.

Mishra, R. (1999), *Globalization and the Welfare State*, Cheltenham: Edward Elgar.

Mlinar, Z. (1992), *Globalization and Territorial Identities*, Aldershot: Avebury.

Morgan, K. O. (1992), *The People's Peace: British History 1945-1990*, Oxford: Oxford University Press.

Morris H. L. (1969 [1921]), *Parliamentary Franchise Reform in England from 1885 to 1918*, New York: AMS Press.

Mullan, P. (2000), *The Imaginary Time Bomb: Why an Ageing Population Is Not a Social Problem*, London: Taurus.

Mulley, G. P. (1997), 'Myths of Ageing', *The Lancet* 350: 1160-61.

National Pensioners' Convention (1998), *Pensions Not Poor Relief*, London: NPC.

Neugarten, B. (1974), 'Age Groups in American Society and the Rise of the Young Old', *Annals of the American Academy of Political and Social Science* 415: 187-198.

Office of National Statistics (1998), *Population Trends 91*, London: HMSO.

OPCS (1991), *Census Report: Historical Data*.

OPCS (1993), *Population Trends* 72: 44-50.

Opinion Leader Research (1999), *Policy-Making in the 21st Century: Engaging the Public*, London: Opinion Leader Research.

Overbeek, J. (1974), *History of Population Theories*, Rotterdam: Rotterdam University Press.

Overbeek, J. (ed) (1977), *The Evolution of Population Theory*, Westport Connecticut: Greenwood Press.

Pampel, F. (1998), *Aging, Social Inequality, and Public Policy*, Thousand Oaks: Pine Forge Press.

Pampel, F. and J. B. Williamson (1989), *Age, Class, Politics, and the Welfare State*, Cambridge: Cambridge University Press.

Park, A. (1999), 'Young People and Political Apathy' in (eds) R. Jowell, J. Curtice, A. Park, K. Thomson, L. Jarvis, C. Bromley and N. Stratford, *British Social Attitudes, 16th Report*, Aldershot: Ashgate, pp. 23-40.

Park, A. (2000), 'The Generation Game' in (eds) R. Jowell, J. Curtice, A. Park, K. Thomson, L. Jarvis, C. Bromley and N. Stratford, *British Social Attitudes*, London: Sage, pp. 1 –21.

Parsons, J. (1977), *Population Fallacies*, London: Elek Books.

Pedersen, S (1993), *Family, Dependence and the Welfare State 1914-1945*, Cambridge: Cambridge University Press.

Pensioners' Charter, (1998), leaflet, October.

Phillipson, C. (1982), *Capitalism and the Construction of Old Age*, London: Macmillan.

Phillipson, C. (1991), 'Inter-generational relations – conflict or consensus in the 21st century', *Policy and Politics* 19(1):27-36.

Phillipson, C. (1998), *Reconstructing Old Age*, London: Sage.

Phillipson, C. and A. Walker, (eds) (1986), *Ageing and Social Policy: A Critical Assessment*, Aldershot: Gower.

Pickard, S. (1998), 'Citizenship and Consumerism in Health Care: A Critique of Citizens' Juries', *Social Policy and Administration* 32(3):226-244.

Pilch, M. and V. Wood (1979), *Pension Schemes*, Aldershot: Gower.

Pratt, H. J. (1976), *The Gray Lobby*, London: University of Chicago Press.

Pratt, H. J. (1993), *Gray Agendas*, Ann Arbor: University of Michigan Press.

Pratt, H. J. (1995), 'Seniors' Organizations and Seniors' Empowerment: An International Perspective', in (eds) D. Thursz, C. Nusberg and J. Prather, *Empowering Older People: An International Approach*, London: Cassells, pp. 53-82.

Preston, S. H. (1984), 'Children and the elderly in the US', *Scientific American* 251(6):44-49.

Quadagno, J. and D. Street (1996), *Aging for the Twenty-First Century*, New York: St. Martin's Press.

Rees, A. (1996), 'T. H. Marshall and the Progress of Citizenship', in (eds) Bulmer, M, and A. Rees, *Citizenship Today: The Contemporary Relevance of T. H. Marshall*, London: UCL Press.

Robertson, R. (1992), *Globalization: Social Theory and Global Culture*, London: Sage.

Roche, M. (1995), 'Rethinking Citizenship and Social Movements: Themes in Contemporary Sociology and Neoconservative Ideology', in (ed) L. Mahen, *Social Movements and Social Classes: The Future of Collective Action*, London: Sage, pp. 186-219.

Royal Commission (1949), *Report of the Royal Commission on Population* (Cmd 7695), London: HMSO.

Royal Commission on Long Term Care (1999) *Final Report. With Respect to Old Age: Long Term Care – Rights and Responsibilities* (Cm 4192-I), March 1999.

Sampson, A. (1971), *The New Anatomy of Britain*, London: Hodder and Stoughton.

Slater, D. (1998), *Consumer Culture and Modernity*, Cambridge: Polity Press.

Stansfield, R. (1993), *Pensioners' Voice*, January/February.

Stears, G. (1998), *Issues Concerning UK Pensions Policy*, Association of British Insurers, Occasional Paper (1), London: ABI.

Steele, D. (1999), *Goodtimes*, October-November.

Steenbergen, B. van (1994), *The Condition of Citizenship*, Sage: London.

Tarrow, S. (1994), *Power in Movement: Social Movements, Collective Action and Politics*, Cambridge: Cambridge University Press.

Thane, P. (1989), 'Old Age: Burden or Benefit', in (ed) H. Joshi, *The Changing Population of Britain*, Oxford: Blackwell, pp. 56-71.

Thurow, L. C. (1996), 'The birth of a revolutionary class', *New York Times Magazine*, 19 May, pp. 46-47.

Titmus, R. (1974), *Commitment to Welfare*, London: George Allen and Unwin.

Tocqueville, Alexis de (1966 [1835, 1840]), *Democracy in America* (ed) J.P. Mayer and M. Lerner; (translation) G. Lawrence, New York: Harper & Row.

Townsend, P. (1957), *The Family Life of Old People: An Inquiry in East London*, London: Routledge and Kegan Paul.

Townsend, P. (1999), *New Pensions for Old: The Key to Welfare Reform*, Tribune pamphlet, ISBN: 0-86292-491-X.

Townsend, P. (2000), letter to the *Guardian*, 11 May.

Townsend, P. and D. Wedderburn (1965), *The aged in the welfare state: The interim report of a survey of persons aged 65 and over in Britain, 1962 and 1963*, London: Bell.

Twine, F. (1994), *Citizenship and Social Rights: Interdependence of Self and Society*, London: Sage.

United Nations (1999), *International Year of Older Persons 1999*, website, http://www.unoorg/esa/socdev/iyop/

Van Parijs, P. (1999), 'The Disfranshisement of the Elderly, and Other Attempts to Secure Intergenerational Justice', *Philosophy and Public Affairs* 27(4):292-333.

Victor, C. (1991), *Health and Health Care in Later Life*, Milton Keynes: Open University Press.

Vincent, J. A. (1995), *Inequality and Old Age*, London: University College Press.

Vincent, J. A. (1999), *Politics, Power and Old Age*, Buckingham: Open University Press.

Vincent, J. A., G. Patterson and K. Wale (2000), 'Older People and Politics', *Generations Review* 10(4): 13 –14.

Vincent, J. A., G. Patterson and K. Wale (2001), 'Understanding the Grey Vote', *Generations Review* 11(1): 9 –11.

Wales Pensioner (3), Summer 1999.

Walker, A. (1987), 'The Social Construction of Dependency in Old Age', in (eds) M. Loney et al., *The State or the Market*, London: Sage, pp. 41-57.

Walker, A. (1992a), 'Poverty and Inequality in Old Age' in (eds) J. Bond, and P. Coleman, *Ageing in Society: An Introduction to Social Gerontology*, London: Sage, pp. 229-49.

Walker, A. (1992b), 'Why Britain Needs a Unified Pensioners' Movement', special supplement, *Grey Power Magazine*.

Walker, A. (1996), *The New Generational Contract*, London: UCL Press.

Walker, A. (1997), *Combating Age Barriers in Employment*, European Research Report, Luxembourg: Office of Official Publications of European Committees.

Walker, A. (1998), 'Speaking for Themselves: The new politics of old age in Europe', *Education and Ageing* 13(1):13-36.

Walker, A. and T. Maltby (1997), *Ageing Europe*, Buckingham: Open University Press.

Walker, A. and G. Naegele (eds) (1999), *The Politics of Old Age in Europe*, Buckingham: Open University Press.

Walker, A. and C. Walker, (1997), *Britain Divided: The Growth of Social Exclusion in the 1980s and 1990s*, London: CPAG.

Ward, R. A. (1993), 'The Politics of Old Age', in (eds) J. Johnson, and R. Slater, *Ageing and Later Life*, London: Sage, pp. 332-38.

Warde, A. (1994), 'Consumers, Identity and Belonging: Reflections on some Theses of Zygmunt Bauman', in (eds) R. Keat, N. Whitely, and N. Abercrombie, *The Authority of the Consumer*, London: Routledge, pp. 58-74.

Waters, M. (1997), 'Inequality after Class', in (ed) D. Owen, *Sociology after Postmodernism*, London: Sage, pp. 23-39.

White, Chris. (1987), 'Pensioner Power!' *Golden Age*, October.

Williams, T. M. Hill and R. Davies (1999), *Attitudes to the Welfare State and the Response to Reform*, DSS Research Report 88, London: HMSO.

Wilson, G. (2000), *Understanding Old Age: Critical and Global Perspectives*, London: Sage.

Worcester, R. M. and R. Mortimore (1999), *Explaining Labour's Landslide*, London: Politico's Publishing.

World Bank (1994), *Averting the Old Age Crisis*, Oxford: Oxford University Press.

Index

Affordability 18, 20, 45, 90, 100, 112-13
Age Concern 2, 24, 26, 32, 34, 40, 41-9,
　45n, 51-2, 54-5, 61, 66-7, 74, 95n, 107,
　132, 136, 150
　Age Concern Cymru 42, 43n, 56
　Age Concern Exeter 131, 136
　Age Concern Southwest 39
Ageism 38, 47, 155
　compassionate 72, 99, 103-4, 106-7,
　109, 112, 154
　scapegoat 102-3, 106, 125
Arber, S. and J. Ginn 6, 23, 29, 31-2, 86,
　104, 144, 147
Association of British Insurers 94n, 98
Association of Retired People and Those
　Over Fifty (ARP/O50) 38, 40

Better Government for Older People
　(BGOP) 2, 39, 49, 51, 56, 60-2, 106
Beveridge Report 28-9, 59, 95n
Blair, Tony 59, 64, 69, 71, 88-90, 94, 99-
　100, 122, 134, 138, 143
Bornat, J. 6, 27-30, 32, 84, 144, 147
Bottomley, Peter 24-5, 140-1
British Election Survey (BES) 27, 63-4,
　76-7
British Pensioners' Trade Union Action
　Association (BPTUAA) 2, 29, 31-3,
　51, 97

Castle, Barbara 54, 83-5, 88, 94, 128,
　147
Citizenship 7, 25, 62, 68, 105, 113, 117-
　18, 127-135, 142-3, 153
Class 3, 73, 79, 81, 105, 129-30, 145-6,
　151, 155
　middle 29, 76, 81, 129-30
　working 29, 76, 129-30, 134
　under 142
Conservative (as reluctant to change) 16,
　75, 81, 136-8
Conservative (as political party)
　governments 19, 32-3, 52, 64-5, 86-9,
　92n, 93, 97, 106, 144

manifesto 70, 104-5
ministers 19n, 24, 31n, 83, 94
party 19, 23, 64-5, 68-71, 74-5, 77-8,
　83, 83n, 85-8, 99, 104-5, 126, 137, 139,
　141, 154
voters 64, 75, 77, 144
Constitution 35-7, 42-3, 129, 151
Consumers 38-9, 93, 103, 134, 142
Crime 54, 65-6, 71-3, 107, 138

Debates
　election 23, 68-9
　Millennium Debate of the Age 2, 24,
　43, 43n, 45, 55-6, 132, 136, 150
　Parliamentary 57-8, 57n
Democracy 3-4, 19-20, 25, 35-6, 43, 48,
　53, 62, 118, 126-7, 135-6, 150-1, 153
Demography 5-6, 8, 11-12, 14-15, 17-18,
　20-5, 27, 72-3, 76, 79, 100, 113, 137-8,
　155
Department of Social Security (DSS) 9,
　59-60, 89-90, 90n, 92
Deserving poor 22, 104-6, 124, 128, 154
Devon 50n, 61, 71, 98, 131-2, 136

Early Day Motion (EDM) 46, 57-8, 57n
Elections, 3-4, 13, 16, 27, 38, 45, 89, 95,
　114, 118, 126, 141, 144-5, 153-4
　by-elections 136
　European elections 96
　local elections 78, 95-6
　see General Elections
Electorate 4, 6, 8, 12, 14, 27, 38, 56, 67,
　73, 75, 79-80, 96, 106, 113, 117, 126,
　135, 142, 154 see also Voters
Eurobarometer 139-41
Europe, EU 6, 8, 11-12, 21, 64, 99, 121-
　2, 126, 129, 133n, 139-41, 147, 154,
　156

Field, Frank 92, 100
Focus groups 1-3, 2n, 55, 63, 73, 107-13,
　117, 119, 121-6, 135-6